irst Settlers of
outh Carolina, 1670–1680

gnes Leland Baldwin

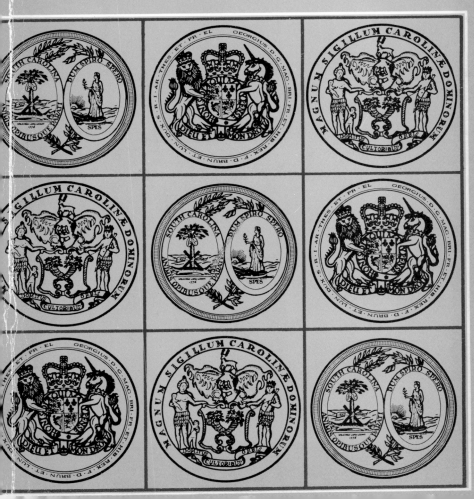

1670   **1970**

This is the first in a series entitled *TRICENTENNIAL BOOKLETS*, to be published by the University of South Carolina Press on behalf of the South Carolina Tricentennial Commission. Other booklets in the series will be announced. The series is part of a scholarly publications program intended to commemorate the founding of South Carolina in 1670.

Two other series published by the University Press on behalf of the Tricentennial Commission will consist of books in hard covers. They are:

1) **TRICENTENNIAL STUDIES**—monographs by various scholars embodying hitherto unpublished research on different aspects of the history of South Carolina. (Number 1, now available, is *The Promised Land: The History of the South Carolina Land Commission, 1869-1890*, by Carol K. Rothrock Bleser.)

2) **TRICENTENNIAL EDITIONS**—new editions of important and inaccessible documents of South Carolina history, with texts established and explanatory introductions provided by modern scholars. (The first volume in this series will consist of two pamphlets by South Carolinians published in London in 1774, edited, with a long Introduction, by Jack P. Greene, who has chosen to publish the resulting book under the title *Bridge to Revolution: The Wilkes Fund Controversy in South Carolina.)*

All three of these series are under the general editorship of the Publications Subcommittee of the Scholarly Activities Committee of the South Carolina Tricentennial Commission.

First Settlers of South Carolina, 1670–1680

Agnes Leland Baldwin

TRICENTENNIAL BOOKLET NUMBER 1

Published for the South Carolina Tricentennial Commission
by the University of South Carolina Press
Columbia, South Carolina

PREFACE

This is a list of settlers of South Carolina in the first decade of her history, 1670–1680, compiled after a thorough and painstaking search of the records noted in the Table of Sources printed on page vii. It does not claim to be a complete list culled from all existing documents that pertain to the period. Other names in other pertinent records can certainly be found. The sources searched are basic ones, however; and the list of names herewith provided is a firm foundation upon which to build.

Although these sources are public records—original manuscripts in the British Public Record Office and the South Carolina Archives, or transcripts and abstracts based on these originals—they contain a great variety of documents. The settlers at Albemarle Point in 1670 were a sophisticated, civilized people, transporting a complex society across the seas. The recording of documents was one of the rudimentary procedures of this society and its complexity is reflected in them.

Two small volumes, dating back to the second year of the colony, show the variety of government business and private interest documented in the public records. The *Journal of the Grand Council* (Source F) reveals that group of men sitting as an advisory body, a legislative assembly, an executive council, and court with civil, criminal, and admiralty jurisdiction. From this Grand Council and the records that it produced have grown all of the legislative and legal institutions of the Province and State of South Carolina and their accompanying records. The second volume, *Records of the Secretary of the Province and of the Register of the Province* (Source C) contains broadly what we would think of today as administrative records and records of private right. The Secretary of the Province performed the functions of the present-day Secretary of State, who is his direct descendant; but during South Carolina's first century he also recorded papers connected with the settling of personal estates, a function of the county judge of probate today. The Register is the ancestor of present-day Registers of Mesne Conveyance and Clerks of Court (in their deed-recording function).

In the first days of the Province the distinctions between the offices of Secretary and Register were not nicely drawn. Sometimes their records are intermixed; at times each can be found recording the same kinds of instruments; and at all times each felt free to indite any document he or a fellow-settler felt to be important. In consequence, we can find in these early records (and the records that evolved from them) documents of many sorts: warrants and grants for land, powers of attorney, commissions, instructions, deeds, administrations, wills, caveats, partnerships, contracts, indentures, shipping notices, business and personal letters, bills of sale, inventories, invoices, shipping permits, quit claims, and mortgages—to mention only a few. (Local birth, death, and marriage notices and church records for this period do not exist.)

The first records concerning South Carolina kept on the other side of the Atlantic show equal variety and complexity. The "Shaftesbury Papers" (Source H) and the *Calendar of State Papers, Colonial* reflect the operations and difficulties encountered in founding the combined business enterprise and imperial colony which the little settlement on the Ashley River was in embryo and came to be in actual fact.

The word "settlers," applied to the persons whose names appear on the following list, is used broadly. It includes not only persons who were present in South Carolina but also some who were simply closely associated with the Province in its early days. In addition to actual settlers, the list contains persons who were granted land but never actually migrated, those who remained only temporarily, and a few such as ship captains, seamen, and merchants, who had strong ties with the Province but may not have become permanent settlers. If a name has appeared at any place in the sources, that name has been added to the list. This provides the historian with a total of 684 persons who must be studied for this first decade in the history of South Carolina.

Five columns of information have been given. The first column contains the name of the settler (with all spelling variations that have been found), the names and number of the members of his immediate family, and his place of residence. Three towns were settled in this period. Charles Towne was on the West bank of the Ashley some ten miles from the open sea; James Towne was on James Island, which borders the West bank of the Ashley somewhat nearer the ocean; and Oyster Point, or New Charles Towne, was established on the point between the Ashley and Cooper rivers.

The second column contains information on the economic or social standing of the settler. The profession or trade, the title (both English or Carolinian), and the position in the local government are provided in this section. No attempt has been made to show exactly when a person acquired a specific title. The date is that of the document from which the information was obtained. A person identified as a "freeman" may have migrated as a "servant."

The third column presents information on the number of servants and slaves that were brought in by each settler. The word "servant" is also a broad one as used in these records. It may mean merely a member of the family or someone whose passage was paid by another person. The word lacks something of the subordinate quality that it now carries.

The fourth column contains the place of origin of each settler, when this information can be gleaned from these records, and the date of arrival in the colony. The largest single group to migrate during this period was those settlers who came in the "First Fleet." The arrival date of the First Fleet most generally accepted is April 1670. A few of those settlers designated "England, First Fleet" actually may have come from Ireland, since the fleet stopped at Kinsale. The list of persons purchasing tickets in

Barbados for Carolina ("J") supplied the date of ticket purchase rather than date of arrival. In many cases this was a return trip from Barbados to Carolina. If no date of arrival was found, the earliest date indicating a person's presence has been shown.

The fifth column contains references to this particular settler in these records. The capital letters refer to the title of sources presented in the Table of Sources. Three periods in a row after a number indicate that additional references appear in subsequent pages.

Because of the scarcity of records, it is impossible to state that this list of persons is complete. Rather than omit data about persons who are not clearly identified, some references are designated with a question mark in parentheses.

It is hoped that the information presented here will serve as a basis for further study of seventeenth-century South Carolina.

TABLE OF SOURCES

Sources A, B, C, F, L, M, and P are published transcripts of original records in the South Carolina Archives.

Sources D, E, and G are unpublished manuscripts in the South Carolina Archives.

Sources H, I, and J contain transcripts of original records in the British Public Record Office.

Source K contains abstracts of records in the South Carolina Archives.

Source O contains abstracts of records in the British Public Record Office.

Source N, an unpublished manuscript in the British Public Record Office, was made in South Carolina in 1765 and sent to England. The "Records of Grants," of which Source N is an abstract, are still in the South Carolina Archives.

Inclusive page numbers at the end of an entry indicate that these are the only pages searched in a source that contains additional pages not pertinent to the years 1670 – 1680.

A. Salley, A. S., ed. *Warrants for Lands in South Carolina, 1672 - 1679.* Columbia: Historical Commission of South Carolina, 1910.

B. Salley, A. S., ed. *Warrants for Lands in South Carolina, 1680 - 1692.* Columbia: Historical Commission of South Carolina, 1915.

C. Salley, A. S., ed. *Records of the Secretary of the Province and the Register of the Province of South Carolina, 1671 - 1675.* Columbia: Historical Commission of South Carolina, 1944.

D. South Carolina Archives, Columbia. "Records of the Register and of the Secretary of the Province, 1675 - 1696, 1703 - 1709." Pp. 1-356.

E. South Carolina Archives, Columbia. "Miscellaneous Records (of the Register of the Province), 1682 - 1690." Pp. 1-386A.

F. Salley, A. S., ed. *Journal of the Grand Council of South Carolina, April 25, 1671 – June 24, 1680.* Columbia: Historical Commission of South Carolina, 1907.

G. South Carolina Archives, Columbia. "Records of the Secretary of the Province, 1675 - 1695." Pp. 1-279.

H. Cheves, Langdon, ed. "The Shaftesbury Papers and Other Records Relating to Carolina and the First Settlement on Ashley River Prior to the Year 1676." *Collections of the South Carolina Historical Society,* vol. 5. Charleston: South Carolina Historical Society, 1897.

I.   Rivers, William James. *A Sketch of the History of South Carolina to the Close of the Proprietary Government by the Revolution of 1719.* Charleston: McCarter & Co., 1856. Pp. 330-470.

J.   Hotten, J. C. *Lists of Emigrants to America, 1600 - 1700.* Reprint. Baltimore: Genealogical Publishing Co., 1962.

K.   Moore, Caroline T., and Simmons, Agatha Aimar, eds. *Abstracts of the Wills of the State of South Carolina, 1670 - 1740.* Columbia: R. L. Bryan Company, 1960.

L.   Salley, A. S., ed. *Warrants for Lands in South Carolina, 1692 - 1711.* Columbia: Historical Commission of South Carolina, 1915.

M.   Salley, A. S., ed. "Abstracts from the Records of the Court of Ordinary of the Province of South Carolina, 1692 - 1700." *South Carolina Historical and Genealogical Magazine,* vols. 8 (1907), 9 (1908), 10 (1909), and 11 (1910).

N.   Public Record Office, London. CO 5/398. Colonial Office, America and West Indies, South Carolina, "An Abstract of the Records of All Grants Made in this Province from the First Establishment . . . to 1765." (Microfilm at Library of Congress, Washington; South Carolina Historical Society, Charleston; and South Carolina Archives, Columbia.)

O.   Sainsbury, W. Noel, ed. *Calendar of State Papers, Colonial Series, America and West Indies, 1669 – 1674.* London: Her Majesty's Stationery Office, 1889.

P.   Salley, A. S., ed. *Commissions and Instructions from the Lords Proprietors of Carolina to Public Officials of South Carolina, 1685 - 1715.* Columbia: Historical Commission of South Carolina, 1916.

CONTENTS

TABLE OF FIRST SETTLERS OF SOUTH CAROLINA, 1670-1680

First Settlers of
South Carolina, 1670–1680

NAME, OTHERS IN FAMILY, TOWN SETTLED IN	OCCUPATION AND TITLE	SERVANTS AND SLAVES	PLACE OF ORIGIN AND DATE OF ARRIVAL	SOURCES
Abercromby, David	Seaman, on *Blessing*		Aug. 1671	A: 7; F: 4
Adams, Ambrose	Servant to Richard Cole		Aug. 1671 on *Blessing*	A: 55
Aggis, Edmund	Freeman			A: 140
Akin, Thomas			May 1674	A: 108; B: 164; E: 355; M: 308
Albert, Ann			Barbados, Spring 1679 on Ship *Mary*	J: 346
Aldridge, Abel				F: 74
Alexander, Richard	Servant to O'Sullivan		England First Fleet on *Carolina*	A: 37,104; H: 134
Allerree, Robert				A: 187
Allouron, Aaron	Servant to O'Sullivan		England First Fleet	A: 37, 104
Andrews, Benjamin Elizabeth Brin	Freeman	2 Servants Arr. 1677	Nov. 1673	A: 77, 197; B: 154; D: 187
Andrews, Walter Wife, Charitie (?)			Aug. 24, 1676	B: 148

Name	Occupation / Status	Holdings	Origin & Arrival	References
Archcraft, Thomas — Wife — Children: 2	Servant, Gunsmith, Freeman by March 1673/74		Barbados Feb. 1670/71	A: 58, 67; F: 7, 8, 46, 51, 69
Argent, William Son, Peter Argent, Born 1668	Servant			F: 42, 43, 49
Ashley, Anthony, Lord (See Shaftesbury)				
Atkins, (Attkins, Adkins) John — Wife, Rachel — James Towne	Gentleman		July 1672	A: 38, 39; C: 53, 54; D: 57, 79
Backwell, William	Servant to Thomas Gray		Feb. or June 1671	A: 27, 28
Baker, Elizabeth	Servant (?), Free Person (Dec. 1679)		Aug. 1671 on *Blessing*	A: 63, 212; L: 56
Banks, Richard — Wife — Children: 9 Quaker	Merchant	1 Negro Man 1 Servant	Jamaica, Feb. 1671 on *Blessing*	B: 37, 138; G: 81, 84, 85; H: 476; J: 440
Bardiner (Bargener), Richard	Servant to John Foster and Thomas Gray		Barbados (?) Feb. or June 1671	A: 28; C: 33, 34; F: 22
Barefoot, Reghmold	Servant to Maurice Mathews		England First Fleet on *Carolina*	H: 135

NAME, OTHERS IN FAMILY, TOWN SETTLED IN	OCCUPATION AND TITLE	SERVANTS AND SLAVES	PLACE OF ORIGIN AND DATE OF ARRIVAL	SOURCES
Barker, Jonathan	Servant to Stephen Bull, Owen's Parliament		England First Fleet on *Carolina*	A: 91; F: 43; H: 134, 176; O: 213
Barley (Borley), John Ran away from England... family of "considerable estate"			England First Fleet on *Carolina*	A: 56; H: 135, 449 (letter); O: 1293
Barnard, George — Wife	Servant to Andrew Percival, Freeman by April 1684		Sept. 1675	B: 128, 153
Barnard, Humphry			Barbados Ketch *Mary & Sarah* Nov. 1679	B: 9; J: 348
Barnes, John	Servant to Richard Cole		Aug. 1671 on *Blessing*	A: 55
Barnet, Lydia				A: 175
Barratt, George	Mariner			A: 183
Barrott (Berrow), Christopher Wife, Elizabeth	Commander of Bark *Adventure* (1678)	Servants	Barbados Nevis "Cittie of Bristol" April 1670 on *Port Royal*	A: 41; D: 59, 61, 65, 113; H: 137, 221, 248, 259, 278, 279; J: 351, 383; O: 434
Barry (Berry), William				F: 38

Name	Occupation	Notes	Origin / Date	References
Barton (Berton, Burton), John Wife, Mary Tosteen	Planter		Barbados (?) Feb. 1670/71	A: 59, 88; B: 110; D: 42, 46, 48, 82, 83; E: 71, 123; M: vol. 10, p. 10; N: 1
Basden, Wentworth				A: 180
Bassett (Bezant, Bessent), John Wife, Lydia James Towne	Cooper		Aug. 1672	A: 59, 100, 101, 178; D: 46; G: 23, 55, 147; L: 43; O:270
Batten (Battin), Richard Wife, Rebecca Charles Towne, Lot 13	Joyner		Before May 1672	A: 147; B: 47; C: 27, 28; D: 59; E: 28A; F: 41, 54, 55, 58
Battin, William Charles Towne			Before 1674	C: 65;
Battison, Julian			Barbados, in the *Endeavor* Oct. 1679	J: 355
Batty, William	Freeman		Before 1674	A: 146; L: 163, 171; N: 4
Bayley, Joan	Servant to Robert Browne		June 1675	A: 114
Bayley (Bailey), Joseph Charles Towne, Lot 9 (held for him by Council)	Captain	4 Servants (Employed by West)	England First Fleet on *Carolina* passenger list	F: 40; H: 136 Held by Spaniards at St. Katherines. Kinsman of Joseph West
Beadon (Bedon), George Wife, Elizabeth Charles Towne, Lots 20, 40	Cooper, Gentleman, Owen's Parliament	5 Servants	Barbados First Fleet	A: 24, 25, 48, 95; B: 176; C: 11, 37, 63; D: 313; E: 75, 80, 83; F: 17, 34, 41; G: 1, 124, 138; H: 137, 176, 204; L: 68, 166; O: 213

NAME, OTHERS IN FAMILY, TOWN SETTLED IN	OCCUPATION AND TITLE	SERVANTS AND SLAVES	PLACE OF ORIGIN AND DATE OF ARRIVAL	SOURCES
Beale, Eusebius	Servant to John Fallock		Mar. 1674	A: 68
Becknal, Jno.	Shipwright		Before Dec. 1679	A: 213
Bedson, Martha	Servant to Nicholas Cartwright		England First Fleet on *Carolina*	H: 135, 169
Benson, Mary Husband, Alexander Oyster Point, Lot 47			Barbados (She left Barbados Oct. 9, 1679, in the *Endeavor* for Carolina) She had been here earlier	A: 130, 132; B: 176; D: 86, J16; J: 354; L: 15, 16; N: 2
Berringer, John		Servants	England First Fleet	A: 86; L: 159, 192, 205
Berringer, Simon		Servants and Negroes	1671 and 1672	A: 84
Berry, Richard			Virginia Dec. 1671	A: 79; C: 64; F: 62; H: 351, 355
Betty, John			May 1674	A: 107
Bevin, William	Servant to O'Sullivan, Freeman by July 1672		England First Fleet	A: 21, 37, 104
Bickerstaffe, Charles died before Sept. 7, 1678				A: 178

Name	Occupation	Place / Date	References
Bidwell, Hugh died before Jan. 20, 1680	Merchant		B: 7; G: 4, 50
Biggs, Timothy Charles Towne, Lot 34	Captain, Merchant, Member of Parliament, Deputy to Earl of Craven in Albemarle (Nov. 21, 1676)	Virginia 1671	A: 129, 132; C: 27, 33, 34; D: 69; F: 30, 41; G: 73; H: 238, 288, 329; I: 318 (?) Biggs's Narrative
Birch, James died before 1677			A: 137
Bird, John Oyster Point connected with Tohill family	Gentleman	Barbados Before Mar. 1678	A: 196, 212; D: 64; E: 77, 147; J: 451; L: 174
Bird, Nicholas		Barbados (?) Feb. 1670/71	A: 91; B: 130; D: 52; E: 50
Bird (Burd), William	Freeman	Before Dec. 1679	A: 212
Bishop, Job died before Mar. 1693 Daughter, Mary	Freeman, Planter		A: 192; B: 162; G: 206; M: vol. 8, p. 172, 197
Blackleach (Blacklidge), Solomon died before 1679	Mariner, Commander of the *James* Frigate	London	G: 3, 4, 48, 50, 59; I: 317; O: 1677-1680, p. 170 (given permission to trade with Spanish, Oct. 22, 1677)
Blewett, Richard	Freeman	Mar. 1679	B: 92

NAME, OTHERS IN FAMILY, TOWN SETTLED IN	OCCUPATION AND TITLE	SERVANTS AND SLAVES	PLACE OF ORIGIN AND DATE OF ARRIVAL	SOURCES
Bodit, Peter died before Feb. 1, 1687 — Wife, Frances	Freeman			A: 167; G: 6
Bodycott (Boydcott, Bodicott, Boddecutt), John died before Jan. 8, 1685 — Wife, Rachel	Freeman, Planter			A: 151; E: 138, 140; G: 182; N: 4
Bonick (Borrick), Thomas	Seaman on *Blessing*			E: 14A; F: 4; G: 76
Bonner (Bonick), Jonathan	Mariner			B: 186; E: 27A, 29; G: 180
Boon, John	Servant to Paul Smith, "Mister" (?)		England First Fleet	A: 48
Boone, John John Boone, Jr.	Ensign, Major, Colonel, Gentleman, Esquire	1 Servant	England First Fleet	A: 20, 48, 63, 78, 122; B: 41, 47, 61, 100, 124, 161; C: 37; D: 32; E: 65, 154, 188, 194, 252, 332; F: 41, 64, 66, 75, 80-84; G: 6, 228; H: 368...; L: 36...; N: 1, 2, 3; P: 35
Boswood, Samuel — Wife, Mary — Daughters, Elizabeth and Margaret Arr. June, 1671 Charles Towne	Servant to John Foster and Thomas Gray, Taylor	1 Servant Ann Workeup Arr. Aug. 1671 Negro, James, Arr. c Sept. 1684	Feb. or June 1671	A: 13, 19, 28; C: 5, 21, 27, 28, 34-35; D: 91; G: 2, 6

Name	Occupation/Status	Slaves and Servants	Origin/Date	References
Bottiley, John	Freeman		Sept. 1678	A: 173; D: 61
Bould (Bolt), Francis died before Oct. 1682 Wife	Gentleman, Esquire (1686)		Before Nov. 1678	A: 190; E: 244; G: 21, 140
Bounden, Jonathan Oyster Point			Before June 1678	A: 164, 168
Bowman, Will	Deputy for Lord Craven		Left ship in Ireland April 1670 on *Carolina*	H: 135; O: 97, 106, 250
Braidy, Philip Wife, formerly Sarah Milner	Servant, Freeman by 1683/84		Dec. 1671	A: 72; B: 139; D: 135; E: 16A, 342; N: 2
Braine, Elizabeth			Barbados (?) Feb. 1670/71	A: 56
Braine (Bryant, Brayne), Henry died before July 25, 1682 Charles Towne, Lot 30	Captain, Mariner, Master *Carolina*	1 Negro man 3 Christian Servants 1 Overseer brought out of Virginia	Barbados First Fleet Was at Cape Fair earlier.	A: 124; B: 50; C: 9, 18; F: 36, 40; G: 6, 107, 153; H: 60...; I: 345
Brett, William				E: 205; G: 67
Bristoll, John				A: 194; E: 357; G: 36
Bristow, John died before 1682	Captain, Merchant			D: 133; G: 37; L: 170, 178; N: 2

NAME, OTHERS IN FAMILY, TOWN SETTLED IN	OCCUPATION AND TITLE	SERVANTS AND SLAVES	PLACE OF ORIGIN AND DATE OF ARRIVAL	SOURCES
Brockhurst (Brockus, Brockhus), William Wife, Sarah Pope Arr. 1678 as Servant Oyster Point	Planter, Mariner	2 Servants Arr. c. Dec. 26, 1683	Barbados	A: 81, 115, 134, 168, 177, 181, 184; B: 82; D: 59, 112, 113, 114, 119 (Partnership and list of goods); E: 65, 128, 240; G: 4; L: 156, 158; N: 2
Brodie, Deoniz				A: 203
Brooks, Robert				G: 35
Brotherhood, Mary	Free Person		Aug. 1671 on *Blessing*	A: 47, 190
Brown, Clement	Freeman			A: 176; B: 25; E: 252
Brown (Browne), Robert Wife	Captain, Merchant (Sept. 1674),Grand Council (1677)	5 Servants 1 Negro	Aug. 1672	A: 30, 110, 114; F: 76, 82
Browne, Bartholomew			Barbados (?) Feb. 1670/71	A: 107
Bryan, James			Aug. 1671	A: 63
Bulkley (Buckley), Charles Oyster Point	Planter			A: 157, 159, 199; D: 83, 109, 144; E: 128
Bulkley, Phillip Oyster Point	Planter, Glazier			A: 157, 159; D: 109; E: 378; M: Vol. 10, p. 214

Name	Occupation / Status	Servants	Origin / Arrival	References
Bull, Burnaby	Captain		England First Fleet on *Carolina*	A: 12, 124; H: 134; L: 59, 206
Bull, Stephen Charles Towne, Lots 24, 25	Captain, Surveyor, Gentleman, Esquire, Grand Council, Lord Proprietor's Deputy (1673)	9 Servants	England First Fleet on *Carolina*	A: 5, 6, 70, 91; B: 12, 21, 50, 59; C: 8, 52; D: 22, 221; E: 248; F: 3-10, 12-14, 16-21, 26-31, 33-36, 38-40, 42-47, 49-61, 70-80, 82...; G: 101 (Ship *Success*); H: 134...; L: 60...; N: 1, 3; O: 97...; P: 7...
Bullen (Bullein), John Oyster Point, Lot 14	Gentleman		Before Mar. 1677	A: 139, 153, 196; D: 87; E: 25A, 81, 97, 153, 196; G: 222, 242; L: 138; N: 1
Burgen, Henry	Servant to John Rivers		England First Fleet on *Carolina*	H: 135
Burges, William	Servant to Joseph Dalton		England First Fleet	A: 24
— Burke (Bourke), Mrs. Pricilla Michael and John Burke Charles Towne, Lot 28			Barbados (?) Feb. 1670/71	A: 38, 44, 109; C: 45, 46, 47; F: 41; L: 123, 189
Burne (Boorne), Andrew	Servant to Thomas and Paule Smith		England First Fleet on *Carolina*	A: 48; C: 50; H: 135
— Burnett, Elinor A widow (1672) she married Thomas Williams by 1676 James Towne (1672)			Before June 1672	A: 12, 118

NAME, OTHERS IN FAMILY, TOWN SETTLED IN	OCCUPATION AND TITLE	SERVANTS AND SLAVES	PLACE OF ORIGIN AND DATE OF ARRIVAL	SOURCES
Burnett, Joane	Servant to John Foster and Thomas Gray (3 years)		Barbados Feb. 1670/71 on *Carolina*	C: 25; H: 253, 271
Burroughs, John	Servant to Thomas Smith		England First Fleet on *Carolina*	H: 134
Bushell, Nicholas Kinsman of Richard Batten	Planter, Clothworker		Aug. 1671 on *Blessing*	A: 14; C: 30-31; D: 77
Bushell, Timothy Oyster Point			Before Feb. 1673	A: 153; B: 26, D: 52
Butler, Richard — Wife, Cicily — Daughter, Mary M. Hickman — Son, John	Planter		Before Mar. 1678	A: 152; E: 244, 247, 272; K: 38; L: 121
Butler, Thomas — Wife, Sarah — Son, Shem — Daughter, Ann Arr. Sept. 1675 Charles Towne	Ship Carpenter	5 Servants	Redriffe near London Aug. 1672	A: 49, 72, 112; C: 36, 37-39, 43-44, 64-66, 70; E: 163; F: 65; G: 163; H: 438; L: 87, 120, 166, 168; N: 2, 3; O: 1294
Buzard, Samuel	Taylor, Servant to J. Foster and Thomas Gray (2 years)		Barbados Feb. 16, 1671 on *Carolina*	H: 253

Name	Status/Occupation	Origin/Date	References
Bydall, Thomas	Servant to Jacob Wayte	Sept. 1675	A: 104
Calfe, Joseph —Wife, Elizabeth Oyster Point, Lot 14	Sword Cutter	c. 1679	A: 199; D: 143; E: 19A, 20A, 23A, 45, 85, 280
Cantey, George —Wife, Martha Son, John Cantey Oyster Point	Planter	by June 1671	A: 29, 30, 163; C: 28; D: 88; F: 36; G: 5, 47, 65; H: 302...; L: 77, 88, 181, 191
Cantey, Teige died before Sept. 1674 —Wife, Elizabeth Sons, William and George Daughters, Mary Smericke and Catherine Maner		Aug. 1672	A: 28, 86, 171; G: 56, 61, 62 Inventory; L: 77
Cantey, William	Freeman	England First Fleet	A: 204; L: 138...
Canting, Dennis		Barbados Mar. 1678 Ship *Mary*	J: 357
Car, William			H: 137...
Carmichael, John	Servant to Joseph Bayley	England First Fleet on *Carolina*	H: 136
Carr, John		England First Fleet	A: 13

NAME, OTHERS IN FAMILY, TOWN SETTLED IN	OCCUPATION AND TITLE	SERVANTS AND SLAVES	PLACE OF ORIGIN AND DATE OF ARRIVAL	SOURCES
Carroll, John — Wife, Mary Smith (1684)	Freeman		Before Sept. 1674	A: 81, 137
— Carter, Eliner			Barbados in the *Joseph and Ann* 1678	J: 357
Carteret (Cartwright), Nicholas and "family" resided in Ickerby (1672)		5 Servants (Apparently did not remain)	England First Fleet on *Carolina*	A: 125, 190; F: 36; O: 97
Carterett (Cartwright), Hugh died before March 1693 Wife, Arr. Aug. 1671 Widow, Ann, later married Daniel Bullman Old Charles Towne, Lot 18	Ensign, Cooper, Owen's Parliament (1670)	1 Servant	Barbados April 1670	A: 24, 25, 80; B: 33, 81; F: 34, 37, 40, 41; G: 38, 39 (contract), 124; H: 137...; K: 3, 28; M: 32; O: 213
Carterett, James Son of Sir George C.	Captain, Landgrave (1671)			H: 270...; O: 429
Carver, Mrs. Joan — Daughter, Margaret Sullivan		1 Negro	Aug. 1672	A: 72, 86; D: 29; E: 369A; G: 23
Cason, William	Servant to William Thomas (1675), Planter Freeman by May 1674		Jamaica (?) May 1673	A: 61, 75, 113; D: 71; G: 61; N:

Name	Status / Description	Origin / Date	References
Cater, Thomas		Jamaica (?) Aug. 1672	B: 56; D: 48; G: 245; L: 158, 208, 209; N: 3; O: 100
Cattell, John	Servant to Thomas Butler, Planter (1676)	Aug. 1672	A: 49, 82; C: 39, 44; E: 5, 30; G: 47
Chambers, John	Servant to John Coming, Carpenter	Aug. 1671 on *Blessing*	A: 45, 92, 94, 197; B: 4, 10; D: 94; F: 33, 73; H: 329...; N: 1
Chambers, William	Servant to Joseph Dalton, Planter (1680), Mariner, Captain (1681)	England First Fleet on *Carolina*	A: 24, 126; D: 81, 115, 147; G: 114; H: 134; N: 3
Chaplin, John — Wife, Ann — Near New Towne Creek	Servant to Capt. John Godfrey, Freeman by Jan. 1678/79	Apr. 1672	A: 4, 198; D: 155; E: 84; L: 140, 160
Chapman, Lawrence	Seaman on *Blessing*		F: 4
Chapman, Richard — Charles Towne, Lot 38 — James Town (1672)	Member Parliament (1672), Merchant	New York(?) Before Apr. 1672	A: 43; C: 14, 42, 43, 48, 50-51, 64; F: 30, 41; H: 391
Christopher, Otho	Servant to Thomas Butler	Aug. 1672	A: 49
Churne, Anthony — Wife, Elizabeth — Sons, Anthony, Tho., Richard, John — Daughter, Frances — Albemarle Point	Freeman, Planter (1672), Owen's Parliament	Before July 1670	A: 36, 41, 56, 94, 97, 118; C: 5; D: 68, 72; F: 13, 34, 73; H: 137...; M: Vol. 9, p. 196
Clark, Jeremiah		Barbados on *Joseph 1678*	J: 357

NAME, OTHERS IN FAMILY, TOWN SETTLED IN	OCCUPATION AND TITLE	SERVANTS AND SLAVES	PLACE OF ORIGIN AND DATE OF ARRIVAL	SOURCES
Clark, Thomas	Apothecary	3 Servants arr. c. Sept. 1683	Apr. 1671	A: 56; B: 148; E: 162, 221; H: 30, 329; J: 476
Clarke, William Wife, Abigail Daughters: 2 Oyster Point	"Physition", "Chyregeon"		Before Apr. 1678	A: 155; B: 129; G: 133, 206, 242 (Will); J: 463, 475
Clay, Steven	Captain, Mariner, Commander Bark *Joseph*		Before Sept. 1676	A: 115; D: 59, 65, 93; G: 1, 78; J: 357
Clement, Henry			Sept. 1675	B: 69
Clerke, Marie	Servant		England First Fleet on *Carolina*	H: 136; O: 97
Clouter, Thomas	Freeman, Mariner, Captain, Gentleman		New England Before Mar. 1679	A: 210; B: 24, 65, 194; D: 106, 136; E: 123, 128, 129A, 339; G: 132; K: 16
Clutterboake (Clutterbuck), Thomas Took part in William Hilton's voyage (1663)	Lieutenant	2 Servants Arr. Feb. 1671	Barbados Before Feb 1671	A: 15; C: 23; F: 36; H: 29, 30
Clutterbuck, John			Before Dec. 1676	A: 120, 121; N: 1, 2, 3
Clutterbuck, Mary	Widow of Barbados (1672)			D: 52

Name	Status / Occupation	Servants	Origin & Arrival	References
Cockfield, William	Servant to George Beadon, Freeman (1673)		England, First Fleet	A: 48, 65
Cole, John	Servant		Barbados, Feb. 1670/71 on *Carolina*	A: 85; H: 358
Cole, Richard, died before 1677, Charles Towne, Lot 42	Carpenter, Shipwright, Member of Parliament (Apr. 1672)	11 Servants	First Fleet	A: 22-24, 45, 55, 147; B: 146; E: 47, 61, 335; F: 14, 15, 17, 30, 34, 41, 65; H: 141...; O: 746
Cole, Robert, Wife, Susanna, Wife, Joanna	Freeman		Before Oct. 1678	A: 181, 183; D: 155; L: 156...
Colleton, James, Brothers, Peter & Thomas, Oyster Point	Esquire, Landgrave, Governor (1686)		Barbados, Before May 1672	A: 3-5, 16-17, 144, 150, 170, 203; B: 3, 17, 18, 19, 22; D: 34; E: 55; G: 2; H: 5, 6, 8...; I: 320; L: 41, 174, 201; N: 2; O: 721; P: 3...
Colleton, Sir Peter, Son of Sir John Colleton, Lord Proprietor, Charles Towne, 9 acres, Oyster Point, Lot 80	Baronet, Landgrave, Lord Proprietor and High Steward, Owner of Fairlawn and Cypress Barony		Barbados, County of Middlesex, Before May 1672	A: 3, 4, 16, 17, 144, 155, 164, 209; B: 17...; C: 8, 9, 12, 32, 59; D: 54, 71, 94, 129, 130, 191; E: 23A, 25A, 360, 364; G: 171, 263; H: 15...; L: 9...; O: 79; P: 3...
Colleton, Thomas, Oyster Point	Landgrave, Colonel, Part owner of the *John and Thomas*		Barbados, Before May 1672	A: 3, 4, 16, 17, 144, 171, 176, 177, 203; B: 17, 18, 19, 106; C: 10, 18, 24, 57, 58; E: 73; H: 16, 125...; N: 1, 2, 4; O: 91; P: 219...

NAME, OTHERS IN FAMILY, TOWN SETTLED IN	OCCUPATION AND TITLE	SERVANTS AND SLAVES	PLACE OF ORIGIN AND DATE OF ARRIVAL	SOURCES
Collins, John of Kaawah	Freeman, Marshall of Keyawah		Barbados Before 1671	A: 136; B: 112; C: 10, 11; E: 106; H: 175, 206...; J: 359, 489; L: 197, 210; O: 245, 284
Collins, Robert Wife, Elizabeth Daughter, Elizabeth			Before Sept. 1678	A: 179; L: 136
Comerton, Philip Charles Towne (no lot number)			Barbados (?) Feb. 1670/71	A: 11, 29; C: 59, 60; F: 41; H: 340
Coming, John Wife, Affra Charles Towne, Lot 29 Oyster Point	Mate on *Carolina*, Mariner (1680), Captain, Gentleman (1678), Esquire (1692), Lord Proprietor's Deputy	7 Servants	England First Fleet	A: 22, 23, 45, 82, 189; B: 20, 40, 47, 146, 154; C: 25, 61, 62, 63, 66; D: 99, 118, 212; E: 26A, 361; F: 29, 34, 40-45, 46, 49, 58; H: 141, 143; J: 30; K: 20 (Will); N: 1, 2; O: 278; P: 33...
Conant, Richard James Towne	Captain (1677), Parliament (1672), Grand Council, Lord Proprietor's Deputy to Earl of Clarendon (1677), Gentleman	1 Negro	New York (?) Before Apr. 20, 1672	A: 20, 89...; D: 75, 92, 155; E: 39; F: 30, 31, 33-35, 37-39, 41-42, 49-57, 59, 60, 63-66, 68-75, 77-82; I: 316, 379, 382; N: 1; P: 8...
Conway, George	Commander of Ketch *Mary and Sarah* (1679)		Before Apr. 1678	A: 156, 191; J: 348, 414
Conway, John	Freeman		Before Apr. 1678	A: 156

Name	Status / Occupation	Origin / Date	Servants	References
Cook (Cooke), William	Freeman, Cooper	Before May 1677		A: 135; B: 161; C: 63; G: 35; L: 61
Cooke, John	Servant to Richard Cole	Aug. 1671 on *Blessing*		A: 55; F: 14
Cooper, Mary	Servant to Robert Daniels	Barbados Apr. 1679 on Ship *Mary*		J: 358
Cottingham, John Oyster Point New Charles Towne (1680), Lot 38	Planter			A: 198; B: 14, 21, 40, 47, 146; D: 80, 109, 133, 179; E: 28A, 32, 76, 87; G: 6, 21, 97; K: 29; M: Vol. 9, p. 203; N: 2
Cowen, John Wife, Judith Arr. Sept. 5, 1682	Freeman, Sawyer	c. 1679		A: 205; B: 169, 170, 171; D: 57, 143; L: 76...; N: 2
Cragwell, Godfrey				G: 53
Crossley (Crossland), Richard	Servant to Richard Cole, set free for idleness (1671)	England First Fleet		A: 23; F: 42; H: 204
Cullpeper, John Wife, Judith Arr. Dec. 1671 Charles Towne, Lot 35	Surveyor General, Parliament (1672)	Barbados Feb. 1670/71	1 Negro 1 Servant	A: 16, 53, 54; C: 5, 11, 14, 23, 32-33, 35, 37, 42, 43, 49, 52, 56, 57, 67-69; F: 5, 13, 30, 41, 60, 61, 67, 68; H: 274; I: 329
Currle, Elizabeth	Servant to Maurice Mathews	England First Fleet on *Carolina*		H: 135
Dale (Deal), Edward	Servant to Richard Cole (1671), Planter (1677)	Aug. 1671 on *Blessing*		A: 55; B: 23; D: 59, 77; G: 6, 168

NAME, OTHERS IN FAMILY, TOWN SETTLED IN	OCCUPATION AND TITLE	SERVANTS AND SLAVES	PLACE OF ORIGIN AND DATE OF ARRIVAL	SOURCES
Dale, John	Servant to O'Sullivan		England First Fleet on *Carolina*	A: 37, 104
Dalton, Joseph	Gentleman, Grand Council, Secretary of the Province, Esquire, Lord Proprietor's Deputy to Sir George Carteret (1672)	7 Servants	England First Fleet on *Carolina*	A: 23, 24, 94, 96; B: 47, 158; C: 6, 39, 45...; F: 15, 20, 23, 34, 41, 50, 64, 66, 68, 71, 72, 73, 74, 75-81; H: 354, 355...
Daniel, Robert Wife, Dorothy Oyster Point	Deputy Governor (1716), Mariner (1679), Gentleman, Esquire, Major (1694), Commander of the *Daniel*, Lord Proprietor's Deputy, Grand Council, Landgrave (1698)		Barbados Before Apr. 1677, Return trip on *Mary* Spring 1679	A: 132, 165; B: 77, 146; D: 102, 245; E: 91, 95, 280, 283; G: 4, 131, 164; J: 280; L: 23...; P: 35...
Darby, Walter	Freeman			A: 117
Darkenwell (Dartnell?), Nathanyell	Servant (?)		England First Fleet on *Carolina*	A: 34; H: 136
Darkenwell, Sampson			England First Fleet on *Carolina*	H: 136 Apparently never arrived
Davice, William	Servant to John Foster and Thomas Gray			C: 25
David, Edward			England	S.C. Historical Magazine, Vol. 37, p. 139

Name	Occupation/Status	Servants	Origin/Arrival	References
Davies, Ralph				A: 171; N: 2
Davies (Davis), Willian —— Wife, Eleanor —— Daughter, Jane —— Son-in-law, Capt. Robert Gibbes Oct. 24, 1678, in Barbados	Lieutenant, Captain, Gentleman	2 Servants (Elizabeth Fee and Elizabeth Maner)	Barbados	A: 168, 184; B: 82; D: 112-114 (Partnership); E: 167, 234; H: 27...; J: 460, 468, 471, 489; L: 140, 162, 190
Davis, Elizabeth				A: 182
Davis, Peter			Barbados Ketch *Joseph* (1679)	J: 364
Dawson, John	Servant to Joseph Dalton, Turner		England First Fleet on *Carolina*	A: 24; H: 134
Denham, Robert				C: 65
Derling, David	Servant to Thomas Lane		Jamaica (?) May 1673	A: 64, 75
Deyos, Richard Charles Towne, Lot 19	Seaman on *Carolina*	1 Servant	England First Fleet	A: 55; D: 68; F: 34, 40; H: 141...
Dickinson, Mrs. Dorcas				D: 52
Dickinson (Dixon), Thomas —— Ann Dickinson, Was appointed Lawful Atty. by Thomas Dickinson	Planter, Gentleman, Second to Shaftesbury on Commission for Trade (1677-79)	8 Servants	Sept. 1675	A: 108; B: 32, 105, 143; D: 108; E: 156, 303, 305; G: 195; H: 2

NAME, OTHERS IN FAMILY, TOWN SETTLED IN	SERVANTS AND SLAVES	OCCUPATION AND TITLE	PLACE OF ORIGIN AND DATE OF ARRIVAL	SOURCES
Dimmoche (Dimock), Elizabeth		Servant to O'Sullivan	England First Fleet on *Carolina*	A: 37, 104; H: 134
Ditty, Richard		Grand Council (Aug. 1673-Feb. 1673)		D: 52; F: 62-66
Doe, Edward		Seaman	England First Fleet	F: 4
Donahee, John		Freeman		A: 146; G: 59, 65; N: 1
Donahue (Donaghoe), James Born 1644 Wife, Priscilla Oyster Point		Planter	Barbados (?) Feb. 1670/71	A: 29, 74, 164, 208; D: 82; F: 71; G: 47; H: 340; L: 88, 89
Donne (Donn), Robert Wife, Elizabeth Arr. 1671 2nd Wife, Mrs. Jane Rixam Charles Towne		Owen's Parliament, Servant to Stephen Bull, Captain, Gentleman, Parliament (1672), Lord Proprietor's Deputy	England First Fleet on *Carolina*	A: 51, 94, 208; C: 13, 43, 44, 51; D: 30, 40, 41, 124; E: 68, 79, 85, 123, 280, 324; F: 7, 14, 30, 37, 39, 74, 75-80; G: 37, 44, 48, 76, 188; H: 134...; N: 1; O: 433
Dowden, Joseph His boy, John Griffin			Barbados Before Nov. 21, 1671	C: 11-13, 19-21, 34, 35, 49; F: 17; H: 339...
Dowling, Mathew died before 1674 Charles Towne		Planter		F: 71; K: 1 (Will)

Downing, Thomas Wife, Elizabeth Son, Thomas, Jr.		A: 209
Drayton, Thomas Planter Owned property on south side of New Towne Creek	of Barbados 1678 Spring (1679) Ship *Mary*	A: 159; D: 65; E: 112, 218, 344; G: 98; J: 362, 453; L: 143...; M: Vol. 10, p. 239
Dry (Drye), Robert Sr. died before Feb. 8, 1682 Son and heir, William Dry		G: 5, 12
Dukes, William	Barbados in the *Adventure* 1679	J: 362
Dupeth, David		A: 152
Dupuis, Enoch		A: 152
Dymond, Richard Oyster Point lot (deserted by June 1689)	Master Ship *Providence* (1679)	A: 154; D: 99
Eakins, Thomas		A: 123, 192; B: 165; E: 133; G: 2
Edwards, Christopher Wife, Ann Daughter, Ann Arr. Feb. 1671 Mrs. Margaret Edwards Oyster Point	Servant to Richard Deyos, Planter, Freeman by Mar. 17, 1672 Barbados First Fleet	A: 15, 32, 55, 58, 173, 175; D: 57, 81, 101, 115, 124, 146; F: 34

NAME, OTHERS IN FAMILY, TOWN SETTLED IN	OCCUPATION AND TITLE	SERVANTS AND SLAVES	PLACE OF ORIGIN AND DATE OF ARRIVAL	SOURCES
Ellis, John — Wife Children, John and James	Planter		1676	A: 199; B: 3; E: 112, 311; G: 98; L: 124, 153, 163; N: 4
Ellis Roger Charles Towne	Shopkeeper		St. Michalls Barbados Before Sept. 1675	C: 64-66, 70, 71
Ellis, Thomas	Servant to John Godfrey		Barbados (?) Feb. 1670/71 on *Carolina*	A: 78, 97; G: 38, 39
English, Mathew	Servant to John Godfrey, Victualler, Provost Marshall, Planter (1682), Freeman by Oct. 1673	1 Servant	Barbados ? Feb. 1670/71 on *Carolina*	A: 66, 78, 97, 139; E: 153, 244, 334; G: 38, 39, 105, 133, 204, 226; N: 1
Erpe (Yarpe), Sarah — Eliza Erpe — Mrs. Mary Erpe Oyster Point, Lot 37			England First Fleet; Arr. Free 1677 on *Carolina*	A: 184; B: 59; D: 141; H: 136; N: 2; O: 97
Evans (Evance), Edward Oyster Point	Freeman, Cordwayner		Barbados on Pink *Neptune* July 21, 1679	A: 126; D: 121, 124; J: 366
Evans, Randall	Servant to Edward Mathews, Mariner (1679)		Aug. 1671 on *Blessing*	A: 113; G: 53; L: 232

Name	Occupation / Status	Servants	Origin / Date	References
Faggs, William	Servant for 2 years			C: 28
Fallock, John Wife and 4 children	Ship Carpenter, Grand Council (1674)	4 Servants	Mar. 1674	A: 68; E: 60; F: 71-73
Farrington, John			Barbados (?) Feb. 1670/71	A: 93; B: 49, 52, 55; C: 49, 52, 55; D: 41, 53
Faulkoner (Falconer), John Wife, Ann Sons, John and Henry Arr. 1672 Charles Towne	Planter		Sept. 1670	A: 50, 91, 102, 103; C: 21, 27, 44, 45; D: 20, 108; F: 34, 43; G: 261; L: 3
Ferith, Samuel	Merchant			C: 70
Field, Christopher died before Sept. 1674	Servant to John Maverick			A: 83; F: 52
Finden (Findon), Thomas died before 1682 Wife, Mary Sons, Thomas F., Jr., John and Henry			June 1671	A: 90; B: 10, 49; G: 5; H: 339
Fisher, John He and wife resided St. Gyles Plantation Convicted for murder, sentenced to death Nov. 5, 1683	Captain, Gentleman		Jamaica (?) Before June 1678	G: 44, 82, 194; O: 103, 986

NAME, OTHERS IN FAMILY, TOWN SETTLED IN	SERVANTS AND SLAVES	OCCUPATION AND TITLE	PLACE OF ORIGIN AND DATE OF ARRIVAL	SOURCES
Fitz (Fitch, Fitts), Jonathan Sr. Son (?) Jonathan Fitch Quaker Oyster Point, Lots 27 & 79		Planter	Before Apr. 23, 1678	A: 154, 191; B: 99; E: 22A, 86, 87, 101, 112, 356; G: 12, 38 (Letter); L: 154..., 158...; M: Vol. 10, p. 237 (Jr.)
Fitzpatrick, Bryan		Servant to O'Sullivan	England First Fleet	A: 37, 63, 104; F: 45; H: 338; O: 279
Flavie, William		Servant to John Smith		A: 105, 106
Fleming, Anthony		Servant to Richard Cole	Aug. 1671 on *Blessing*	A: 55
Fleming, James Age 33 (1674)			Ireland	So. Car. Hist. Mag., Vol. 37, p. 94
Fling, Hugh Wife, Aelss Gregge			Jan. 28, 1677	B: 119; L: 6, 186, 213; M: Vol. 10, p. 239
Flinte, Steph.			England First Fleet on *Carolina*	H: 135
Flower, Moses		Servant 2 years	Barbados Feb. 16, 1670/71 on *Carolina*	H: 253

Fluellin, Thomas — Wife, Abigail — 2nd Wife, Jane Colony of James Towne		Dec. 1671	A: 46, 98, 134, 137; G: 173; L: 170
Fogertee, Edmund			A: 19, 86
Fookes (Fowkes), James	Master of Ship *Machetauck* (Aug. 1672)		C: 48; F: 43 Evidently did not settle
Footer, Mrs. Joane		Before Nov. 1679	B: 8
Forgison, John	Servant to Robert Browne	June 1675	A: 114
Foster, John Charles Towne Lots 11, 13	Grand Council, Cassique, Gentleman, Lord Proprietor's Deputy, Purchased a Sloop of 30 tons (Nov. 1671) 4 Servants	Barbados	A: 5, 56, 150, 163; B: 13; C: 25, 27; D: 245; E: 10A; F: 3, 5, 22, 23, 28, 34, 41, 50; H: 339; I: 383 (Inventory); J: 478; L: 117, 160, 232; O: 1101
Fowell, John died before 1682 Brother of Richard Fowell	Merchant, Esquire		D: 103; G: 37, 129
Fowell, Richard died before Jan. 2, 1679 Brother John Fowell willed ½ vessel *Mary* Wife, Saraugh — Widow Sarah Fowell — married Edward Middleton	Gentleman, Esquire, Merchant	Before Nov. 1678	A: 188; B: 13; G: 36, 37, 58 (Will); H: 240; J: 454 (?)

NAME, OTHERS IN FAMILY, TOWN SETTLED IN	OCCUPATION AND TITLE	SERVANTS AND SLAVES	PLACE OF ORIGIN AND DATE OF ARRIVAL	SOURCES
Fowell, Sarah widow of Richard Fowell (?)	Free Person		Before Jan. 25 1678/79	A: 195
Fox, Stephen Phillis Fox	Tanner	1 maid Servant 4 Negro men 4 Negro women 2 Negro boys 2 Negro girls	Barbados Ship *Mary* Spring 1679	B: 56; D: 93, 182; J: 368; L: 118, 175; N: 4
Frank, Rachel	Servant to John Coming		Aug. 1671 on *Blessing*	A: 45
Fraser (Fraiser), John	Servant		First Fleet	A: 98; D: 55
Frezell, Daniell	Freeman		Aug. 1671 on *Blessing*	A: 188; L: 13
Frezer, John John Frezer, Jr.	Servant to O'Sullivan		Aug. 1671 on *Blessing*	A: 37, 105
Frith, Samuel	Merchant		Barbados Before Sept. 1675	C: 65, 70, 71
Frizen (Fraiser), Jo	Servant to Hambleton		England First Fleet on *Carolina*	H: 135
Froman, John				D: 66

Name / Family	Title / Office	Notes	Origin / Date	References
Fuller, William Son, William Fuller (12 in family) Joseph Heape Next of Kin Close friend of Jacob Waight	Esquire, Gentleman, Grand Council		Apr. 1678	A: 210, 213; B: 13, 27, 78, 210, 213; E: 16A, 30; G: 23, 122, 169, 183; L: 50, 67, 182, 185
Gantlet (Gantlett), George	Servant to John Coming		Aug. 1671 on *Blessing*	A: 45; C: 63; L: 124, 126, 171
Gardner, John	Labourer		Before May 1673	A: 63; C: 67, 68; D: 124; F: 36; H: 396
Gaud (Gand), Mary	Servant to Gov. Sayle		England First Fleet	A: 52
Gay, Abel	Captain			F: 55
George, Robert — Wife, Isabell	Planter		Barbados (?) Feb. 1670/71	A: 99, 117, 138; E: 183, 192; L: 160
Gibbes, Robert Brother, Thomas Gibbes His Daughter, Mary Gibbes Bluff Bank or Cow Pen Plantation	Captain, Esquire, Gentleman, Sheriff of Berkeley County (1684), Lord Proprietor's Deputy (1699), Grand Council, Chief Justice, Governor	Several "persons and slaves"	Barbados by Aug. 1672	A: 29; B: 46, 119; C: 55, 56; D: 136; E: 81, 106, 147, 198, 264; F: 44; G: 24, 116, 142, 169, 196, 228; H: 88…; L: 17…; M: Vol. 10, p. 237; N: 2, 3, P: 90…
Gibbes, Thomas Wife, Elizabeth Daughters, Rebecca Golding, Elizabeth, wife of Edward Paty Charles Towne (New)	Captain, Esquire, Gentleman, Justice of Peace		Barbados Before Feb. 1680	B: 30; E: 185, 252; G: 56, 57, 129; K: 13; L: 15

NAME, OTHERS IN FAMILY, TOWN SETTLED IN	OCCUPATION AND TITLE	SERVANTS AND SLAVES	PLACE OF ORIGIN AND DATE OF ARRIVAL	SOURCES
Gibbons, Edmund died Baltimore, Md. before 1686 Brother, Francis Sister, Ann	Merchant		Barbados	A: 115; D: 215, 216
Gibbons, William				D: 101, 115
Gilbert, Benjamin	Servant to William Owens		England First Fleet	A: 56
Gilliard, Richard	Freeman		Barbados (?) Feb. 1670/71	A: 186
Gittes, Henry			Barbados Spring 1679 on Ship *Mary*	J: 371
Godfrey, John Wife, Mary Sons, Capt. John, Richard, & Benjamin Daughter, Mary Davis Charles Towne	Lt. Col., Grand Council, Esquire, Justice of Peace (1683), Deputy Governor (1684), Lord Proprietor's Deputy to Earl of Craven (1671), In business with Colletons	5 Servants Arr. Feb. 1670/71	St. Peters All Saints Parish, Barbados 1670	A: 3...; B: 81, 82, 157, 159, 160, 164, 168, 169; C: 6, 16, 17, 35, 48, 54, 55, 64, 70; D: 97, 134, 135, 237; E: 29, 107, 334, 342, 365; F: 3-4...; G: 2, 3, 7, 23, 38, 39 (contract), 122, 190, 212, 220, 227, 241; H: 29...; J: 371; K: 14; O: 143...

Name	Status / Description	Origin / Date	Servants	References
Godfrey, John, Jr. —Wife, Elizabeth —Daughter of Jane Cliffe* Elizabeth was also the widow of Wm. Neale (1688)	Captain, Gentleman (1688), Esquire	Barbados 1670		A: 97; B: 83; D: 237, 262, 263; E: 323, 369A; G: 114, 126; K: 13; L: 17...; N: 2
Goffe (Gough), Robert —Wife, Elizabeth See Grant Book C, p. 358 for Plat dated 1677		July 1672	2 Servants	A: 48, 148; B: 22, 61; D: 23
Gooden, Robert	Servant (2 years to serve), Yeoman	Before Feb. 1672		B: 24
Gorden, George		Barbados Aug. 1679 on *Plantation*		J: 372; L: 131
Goterr, Mary				D: 59
Gourden, Thomas	Servant to Hambleton	England First Fleet on *Carolina*		H: 135
Greatbeach, Thomas				A: 191; B: 30, 35; E: 54; M: Vol. 8, p. 197
Green, Elizabeth				B: 27; G: 0
Green, James Wife, Lydea	Servant to John Fallock, Planter (1688), Freeman by Dec. 1676	Mar. 1674		A: 68, 121; E: 181, 311, 386A

*See Jane Rixam and Robert Donne

NAME, OTHERS IN FAMILY, TOWN SETTLED IN	OCCUPATION AND TITLE	SERVANTS AND SLAVES	PLACE OF ORIGIN AND DATE OF ARRIVAL	SOURCES
Green, John Daughter, Elizabeth				A: 166; G: 244; L: 130...
Grey (Gray), Thomas Wife, Jane (Jeane) Charles Towne, Lot 10	Serjeant Major (1672), Captain, Grand Council, Lord Proprietor's Deputy to Duke of Albemarle, Overseer to Sir J. Yeamans	In charge of 10 servants for Sir J. Yeamans	Barbados Feb. 1670/71	A: 3, 5, 28; C: 19-21, 25-29; F: 3...; H: 234...; I: 383 (goods listed) O: 278...
Grey, William (Related to Thomas Gray)	Servant to Thomas Gray		Barbados (?) Feb. or June 1671	A: 8, 28
Griggs, Robert Wife, Alice			Barbados Mar. 1678 on Ship *Mary*	J: 370
Gubbs, Thomas	Servant to Nicholas Cartwright		England First Fleet on *Carolina*	H: 135
Hall, Gyles Charles Towne, Lot 12 Barbadian Adventurer	Captain		Barbados Before Sept. 1671	C: 14, 18, 19, 20; F: 7, 41; O: 1101
Halstead, Mathias	Captain of *Blessing* May 1, 1671	1 Servant Henry Leeke, Yeoman	Before May 1, 1671	C: 24, 25, 26, 66; F: 4, 18, 19, 21, 22, 48, 57, 58; H: 318; I: 315, 359, 363, 369; O: 210, 517...

Name	Status/Occupation	Servants	Origin/Arrival	References
Hambleton, (Edward?)	Major	9 Servants	England First Fleet on *Carolina* passenger list	H: 135, 154, 157, 299; O: 97 Apparently he never migrated, and his 9 servants returned
Harbin, Joseph Brother, Alexander	Merchant		Barbados	A: 160; D: 89; E: 363 Evidently did not settle here
Harding, George			of Barbados Dec. 19, 1672	C: 57, 58 (May not have come)
Harding, Katharin	Free Person			A: 186
Harleston, Affra married John Coming			England First Fleet on *Carolina*	H: 134
Harleston, Charles	Freeman			A: 189; B: 26; D: 98
Harris, Joseph Oyster Point	Captain, Commander of Sloop *Endeavor*			F: 53
Harris, Mathew	Servant to Thomas Lane		July 1672	A: 64, 75
Harrison (Harris), Joseph Oyster Point	Clerk		Before Apr. 1679	A: 202; B: 4, 164; D: 112
Hart, Thomas James Towne "An evil member of the Province"	Yeoman		Before June 1672	A: 10; F: 28
Hartley, John died before Apr. 26, 1682 Oyster Point	Servant to Christopher Portman, Taylor, Freeman by April 1677		Aug. 1671 on *Blessing*	A: 109, 113, 133, 163; G: 6, 15

NAME, OTHERS IN FAMILY, TOWN SETTLED IN	OCCUPATION AND TITLE	SERVANTS AND SLAVES	PLACE OF ORIGIN AND DATE OF ARRIVAL	SOURCES
Harvey, Henry Son sent with servants	"Justice", In business with John Stroud	20 Servants in Partnership with John Strode	Barbados Before Nov. 1670	C: 57, 58; H: 216...230, 232
Hatchman, Joseph	Gentleman		Oct. 1678	A: 196; B: 113; E: 268; G: 23, 140; L: 65...
Hatton, William	Cooper			A: 187; D: 155
Hawkes, John				A: 41, 97; D: 68; H: 170; J: 41, 97
Hawkinson, John	Servant to John Smith			A: 106
Hays, Dennis Wife, Mary Son, Michaell	Planter		Before July 1678	E: 55, 274; G: 3, 173, 178; L: 51...
Henshaw, Michael				A: 158; B: 3; D: 155
Hern (Hyrne), Peter Jr. of age by 1677 Mary Hern Bridget Hern Richard Hern Purchased 44 ac. site at James Towne 1686 (?)				A: 145; G: 246

Name	Occupation/Status	Origin/Arrival	References
Herne (Hearne, Hyrne), Peter (Sr.) Son Peter Hern, Jr.	Parliament (1672), Gentleman	Before Apr. 1672; Negro, Warren Arr. May 1682; Negro Woman Arr. Aug. 23, 1683	A: 43, 57, 123, 153, 160; B: 56, 98, 133, 189, 191; D: 65; E: 25A; F: 30; G: 98, 246; N: 3
Hewitt, Mathew	Servant to Maurice Mathews	England First Fleet on *Carolina*	H: 135
Higgs, George	Servant to Thomas Hurt	Aug. 1671 on *Blessing*	A: 34, 68
Hill, Richard	Freeman, Planter	June 1671	A: 126; B: 50, 68; D: 185; E:" 205; L: 55...; N: 2, 4
Hill, William	Servant to Oliver Spencer	June 1671	A: 84; O: 101
Hilton, William	Captain, Commander of Ship *Adventure* (1663)	Barbados 1663	A: 7, 8, 15, 42, 71; C: 10, 18, 23; H: 13...; O: 315
Holford, John	Servant to Thomas Butler	Sept. 1675	A: 112
Hofford, Nicholas	Servant to Christopher Portman	Aug. 1671	A: 113
Hollis, Ed		England First Fleet on *Carolina*	H: 134 Apparently never arrived
Holmes, John	Planter		E: 47; F: 77; J: 479
Holton (Houlton), Thomas Judith, Arr. Aug. 1671	Freeman	Before 1671	A: 10, 31, 94, 140; C: 52, 60; E: 40A; F: 46, 66; G: 188; L: 52, 60

NAME, OTHERS IN FAMILY, TOWN SETTLED IN	OCCUPATION AND TITLE	SERVANTS AND SLAVES	PLACE OF ORIGIN AND DATE OF ARRIVAL	SOURCES
Hooper, John Wife, Ester (Hester dau. of Thomas Lane)	Servant to Thomas Lane, Planter, Viewer of Tobacco, Freeman (1674)		Jamaica May 1673	A: 64, 74, 75, 135; D: 23, 29, 66, 71; F: 79; G: 1; N: 1; O: 99
Hopkins (Hoppins), John	Servant to Lady Margaret Yeamans	1 Servant	Feb. 1672 as a servant Arr. free Jan. 1673	A: 112, 143; B: 67; D: 121
Horton, John died before 1682 Wife, Mary New Charles Towne (1681), Lot 39	Servant to John Fallock, Carpenter, Freeman by Aug. 1677		Mar. 1674	A: 68, 142; B: 158; D: 138; G: 6, 109; N: 2
Houghton (Haughton), Will			England First Fleet on *Carolina*	H: 136 Apparently never arrived
Houndsen (Humdson), Roger Wife, Ann 1 Child			Dec. 1671	A: 74
Howard (Haward), Edward	Servant to Christopher Portman		Aug. 1671 on *Blessing*	A: 113, 203
Howe (How), Millicent	Spinster, Servant to Col. Joseph West, Servant to Will Bowman		London First Fleet on *Carolina*	A: 63; C: 7, 8; H: 135

Name	Occupation/Status	Origin/Arrival	Notes	References
Howell, Evans	Servant to John Foster and Thomas Gray	Barbados (?) Feb. or June, 1671		C: 25; J: 28
Huddlesworth, John (Huddlestone?)	Servant to Thomas and Paul Smith, Servant to Thomas and James Smith, Freeman by Mar. 1677	England First Fleet on *Carolina*		A: 96, 127; E: 60; H: 134
Huggins, Edward	Servant to Robert Brown	Aug. 1672		A: 110, 114
Hughes (Hews, Huges), Henry	Lieutenant, Parliament (1672), Council	Barbados Apr. 1670	½ interest in 1 Servant	A: 17, 22, 23, 30, 82; B: 54; C: 52, 61-63, 65; F: 3-10, 13, 21, 24-30, 36, 40; H: 176
Hughes, John		Feb. 1670/71		A: 100
Hughes, Simon	Servant to Stephen Bull	Aug. 1671 on *Blessing*		A: 5, 70
Humpreys, John	Servant to William Owens	England First Fleet on *Carolina*		H: 135
Humpreys, Thomas		England First Fleet		H: 136
Hunt, Robert	Servant to William Owens, Freeman by Aug. 1677	England First Fleet		A: 56, 141; L: 104, 121
Hunt, Thomas born 1648 Wife, Jane (1677) Wife, Elliner (1679)	Planter, Viewer of Tobacco	May 1673	3 Servants 4 Negroes	A: 62, 109, 113, 141, 211; B: 70; D: 108; E: 110; F: 79; G: 62

NAME, OTHERS IN FAMILY, TOWN SETTLED IN	OCCUPATION AND TITLE	SERVANTS AND SLAVES	PLACE OF ORIGIN AND DATE OF ARRIVAL	SOURCES
Hutton, James of Ittawan Island	Servant, Planter (1680)		Dec. 1671	A: 77; D: 121, 122
Hurt, Thomas (Hurst) Wife, formerly Mary Gorge (1672) Wife, Vera Aura (1680) Charles Towne Lot 61 for Wife James Towne (?)	Gentleman	2 Servants	Aug. 1671 on *Blessing*	A: 34, 68, 69, 209; C: 34, 55, 56; D: 50, 57, 77, 121, 124, 215; E: 147; F: 40, 41, 56; G: 56, 57; H: 379 Needs more research.
Ingram (Ingrum), Thomas Charles Towne, Lot 53	Planter, Owen's Parliament		England First Fleet on *Carolina*	A: 33, 135; D: 23; H: 134, 176; O: 213
Jackson, Margaret died before Feb. 1679 Son Daughter, Margaret Weshett	Spinster, Widow			G: 55, 58 (Inventory)
Jackson, Originall Wife, Millicent (by 1672) Daughter, Sarah	Lieutenant, Carpenter		England First Fleet (?)	A: 46, 102; C: 22; D: 108, 117 (Gift 4 Acs.); E: 283; F: 5, 7, 34, 43, 44; G: 55, 188, 208

Name	Description	Origin / Notes	References
Jackson, William died before Jan. 24, 1684 Son of Elizabeth Jackson, London, England	Servant to William Thomas, Planter (1683)	London, England May 1673 Jamaica (?)	A: 62, 113, 135; E: 283; G: 47, 73, 188 (Will)
Jefford (Jeffors), Amos	Parliament (1672) 4 Servants	Dec. 1671	A: 57, 76, 95; D: 23; F: 30, 34, 36, 42
Jefford, John			A: 149, 174
Jenkins, William	Servant to Nicholas Cartwright	England First Fleet on *Carolina*	H: 135
Jenner, Thomas	Captain of *John and Thomas*	Barbados before Aug. 1672	A: 28, 29; F: 44; G: 155; H: 255, 256; J: 368; O: 364, 430, 433
Jenning, John Quaker		Barbados	G: 39; J: 402 He and his brother returned to Barbados 1679
Jephon, Mrs. Sarah Susanna Jephson		Barbados May 1679	B: 57; J: 380
Jerman, George	Servant to John Godfrey	Barbados (?)	A: 97
Johnson, Adrian	Seaman	England First Fleet	F: 4
Johnson, Edward Wife, Marie			A: 213; B: 8
Johnston, Robert	Major		C: 9

NAME, OTHERS IN FAMILY, TOWN SETTLED IN	OCCUPATION AND TITLE	SERVANTS AND SLAVES	PLACE OF ORIGIN AND DATE OF ARRIVAL	SOURCES
Jones, Ann	Servant to William Thomas		Jamaica (?) May 1673	A: 113
Jones, Evan Wife, Joan Arr. Mar. 1672			Barbados Feb. 1670/71	A: 59, 65, 114; C: 55, 57; J: 80
Jones, Francis died before Sept. 1693 Wife, Mary Sons, Francis, Philip Daughters, Lewry, Mary, Elizabeth, Sarah, Ann	Brasser		Before July 1678	A: 167; G: 140
Jones, Henry died before Nov. 1678	Servant to Thomas and James Smith, Freeman by May 1672		England First Fleet	A: 9, 14, 96, 184; H: 142, 240
Jones, James Wife, Elizabeth Charles Towne, Lot 14	Freeman, Planter, Parliament (1672)		Barbados (?) before Oct. 1672	A: 44, 57, 136; C: 53, 54; D: 112, 134, 325; E: 10A, 35, 50; F: 30, 40; G: 94; J: 381; N: 2
Jones, John	Agent to Sir J. Yeamans, Owen's Parliament		Barbados Apr. 1670	E: 157; G: 238; H: 187; L: 22...; O: 213
Jones, Nathaniel				A: 175
Jones, Phillip	Servant to John Maverick			F: 7

Jones, William Wife, Ann One Child	Servant to William Thomas (1673), Planter	A: 62, 73, 113; B: 46; D: 107; G: 10, 238; H: 435; L: 169; O: 100, 1270
Jordan, Hugh 1674 age ca. 30	"One of first Settlers"	C: 60; So. Car. Hist. Mag., Vol. 37, p. 96
Jourdan, Oliver Wife, Ann Children, Mary and Michaell	Arr. Nov. 1678, in Ship *Pembrook*	B: 118, 133
Kemp, Hamlett New Charles Towne, Lot 46 (Nov. 18, 1680)	Planter Before Apr. 1677	A: 130, 131; D: 26, 116; N: 2
Kennis, William Wife, Joanna Son, William Charles Towne, Lots 16 and 17	England First Fleet on *Carolina*	A: 26, 27; F: 41, 51; H: 136...
Kincade, Robert	Servant to Godfrey Cragwell, Freeman before Feb. 1679	G: 53
Kinder, Susanna	England First Fleet on *Carolina*	A: 18; F: 16, 17; H: 134...
King, Leah Thomas and Leah King		A: 201

NAME, OTHERS IN FAMILY, TOWN SETTLED IN	OCCUPATION AND TITLE	SERVANTS AND SLAVES	PLACE OF ORIGIN AND DATE OF ARRIVAL	SOURCES
King, Thomas	Servant to Oliver Spencer		Aug. 1672	A: 84, 201; H: 134; L: 178
Kinsell, John	Servant to John Williamson		First Fleet	A: 27
Kyrtland, Abenezer				A: 193
Lacy, Daniel died before Sept. 1684 Wife and Child				A: 131
Ladson, Francis Brother, John Ladson	Planter			A: 185; D: 138; E: 33, 57; L: 118, 209
Ladson, John Oyster Point	Merchant, Distiller	2 Negro Men Arr. in Sloop *Betty* 1692	Barbados Aug. 1679 on *Plantacon*	B: 8, 38; D: 91; E: 5, 29, 32, 57, 74, 75, 76, 95, 121; G: 12, 119, 121, 138, 168, 144; J: 385; L: 3, 70, 71
Laford, Thomas				F: 61
Lane, Thomas Wife, Judeth Arr. May 1673 Daughter, Hester married John Hooper	Gentleman	8 Servants	July 1672	A: 64, 75, 135; C: 48, 49; D: 29; F: 43, 58, 59; L: 21

Name	Status / Notes	Origin / Date	References
Lanell, Edith			G: 58
Lapal (?), John			N: 2
Larmouth (Larmott), John	Servant to Stephen Bull	England First Fleet on *Carolina*	A: 6, 70; H: 134
Lashley, Robert	Servant		C: 63
Lawrison (Lorrisson), John Near James Towne	Mariner 1 Servant	1672	A: 19, 116
Lawson, Jane (Joan)	Servant to Joseph Dalton, Spinster	England First Fleet on *Carolina*	A: 24; E: 47, 61, 275; G: 124; H: 134
Layton, Robert Elizabeth Layton	Servant to Edward Mathews (1671), Freeman (1675), Planter (1686)	Aug. 1671 on *Blessing*	A: 111, 113; E: 254, 257; G: 1
Leahe (Leeke), Henry	Servant for 3½ years (1672), Yeoman		C: 24, 25
LeBas, James	Merchant, purchased Joseph West's plantation (1686)		B: 190; D: 194; L: 95; P: 44, 61
Leeds, Robert	Servant to Thomas Lane, Servant to Robert Gouger	July 1672	A: 64, 75, 148
Leigh, Henry			A: 180
Leister (Lister), Edmund Wife, Dorothy	3 Servants	Virginia Apr. 20, 1676	C: 56, 59, 66, 67, 68; G: 40, 41

45

NAME, OTHERS IN FAMILY, TOWN SETTLED IN	OCCUPATION AND TITLE	SERVANTS AND SLAVES	PLACE OF ORIGIN AND DATE OF ARRIVAL	SOURCES
Lewis, Hugh	Servant to Edward Mathews		Aug. 1671 on *Blessing*	A: 113, 141; C: 52; D: 93
Lewis, Robert Wife, Mary Arr. 1675				A: 134, 178; F: 52; G: 186; L: 24, 27, 103, 239
Lilly, Alexander	Servant to Stephen Bull		Apr. 1671	A: 6, 70
Lindon, Joseph			1677	B: 149
Lisster (Lyster), George				A: 145; B: 56
Lockier (Locker), Robert	Servant to Stephen Bull		Aug. 1671 on *Blessing*	A: 5, 70
Lockwood, Nicholas Oyster Point	Captain, Commander Ship *Mary* (1679); Mariner		London (?)	A: 154; B: 11; D: 102, 110, 111, 113; J: 346, 362; L: 6
Loe, William				F: 47, 49, 54, 55; H: 329...
Long, William	Servant to Amos Jefford (1672), Freeman (1675)		Feb. 1672	A: 95, 101
Lorrison, John	Mariner	1 Servant	1672	A: 116
Love, Edward	Freeman			A: 177
Lowell (Lovering, Loving), Michael	Servant to John Coming		Aug. 1671 on *Blessing*	A: 45; D: 107; F: 33; G: 186; H: 329...

Name	Occupation/Status	Servants	Origin	References
Loyde, Jo	Servant to Nich. Cartwright		England First Fleet on *Carolina*	H: 135
Lucas, Samuel	Servant to John Coming		Aug. 1671 on *Blessing*	A: 45; F: 34, 61; H: 395
Lumsden, William	Servant to Hambleton		England First Fleet on *Carolina*	H: 135
Lynch, John died before 1682 Brother, Nicholas	Merchant		Barbados (?)	G: 6, 7, 8, 161, 162
Lynch, Jona (Johna, Jonah) "of Wattesaw als the blessing"	Gentleman, Esquire, Justice of Peace	2 Servants Arr. 1679	Before Apr. 30, 1677	A: 136, 197, 200, 211; B: 16, 143, 144, 161; D: 75, 182, 186, 194; E: 123, 150, 175, 201, 202, 210, 239, 274; G: 6, 84, 85; L: 126, 237; N: 4
Lynch, Nicholas Wife, Alice Brother, John	Mariner		Barbados Galway, Ireland	G: 6, 7, 103, 161; J: 383
Macey, Ann			Apr. 1677	B: 92
Machanellae (Mackanellor), Thomas	Servant to Thomas Butler		Aug. 1672	A: 49, 85; G: 47
McDonald, Neale				A: 192
MacMarvill, Mary Son Oyster Point				A: 133

NAME, OTHERS IN FAMILY, TOWN SETTLED IN	OCCUPATION AND TITLE	SERVANTS AND SLAVES	PLACE OF ORIGIN AND DATE OF ARRIVAL	SOURCES
Magrady, Hugh	Servant to Robert Brown		Aug. 1672	A: 110, 114
Mahone, James	Servant		Barbados Aug. 1679	J: 390
Mahoone (O Mahone), Dennis	Servant to Richard Cole (1670), Planter (1678)		First Fleet	A: 23, 33, 80; D: 66, 104; E: 318; F: 14; G: 23, 58, 172, 186, 249
Man, Miles	Overseer on Lord Ashley's Plantation (c. Jan. 1671/72)			H: 375, 406, 425
Manley, John				N: 1
Mannen, Andrew			Barbados Spring 1679, Ship *Mary*	J: 387
Mare, John	Servant to O'Sullivan		England First Fleet	A: 37, 104
Marshall, James	Owen's Parliament			H: 176
Marshall, Ralph born 1647 Wife, Mary Stock Arr. Nov. 1678 Charles Towne, Lot 8	Gentleman, Grand Council, Lord Proprietor's Deputy		England First Fleet on *Carolina*	A: 27, 43, 75, 91, 94, 146...; B: 110, 130, 131, 183; C: 11, 28, 37-39; E: 73, 95; F: 3...; G: 59, 61, 65; H: 3...; L: 23
Marshe (Marsh), Samuel			Before 1675	C: 65, 70

Name	Occupation/Title	Origin / Arrival	Servants	References
Mathews, Edward Charles Towne, Lot 8	Parliament (1672)	Aug. 14, 1671 on *Blessing*	5 Servants 1 Servant Arr. Aug. 14, 1671	A: 64, 113; C: 43, 44, 51-52; F: 13, 30, 34, 36, 41; H: 329, 350, 408; N: 1; O: 279
Mathews, Elizabeth	Servant to O'Sullivan	England First Fleet on *Carolina*		H: 134
Mathews, Maurice (Morris) died before March 4, 1692 Charles Towne Lots 37 and 54	Major, Esquire, Gentleman, Grand Council, Surveyor General, Lord Proprietor's Deputy to Earl of Shaftesbury (1671)	England First Fleet	4 Servants	A: 94, 123, 144, 170, 185, 188; B: 20, 50, 66, 104, 107; C: 14, 49-50, 52, 66, 69; D: 32, 93, 99, 118, 131; E: 10A, 58, 184, 188, 296, 331; F: 3-10, 12-14, 16, 18- 22, 24-31, 33-36, 38, 39, 40, 42- 46, 50-82; G: 24-34, 36 (Charter of the *Mary*), 102, 107, 118, 120 153, 231; H: 135...; I: 382; L: 19 169; N: 1, 2, 3; Salley, "Narrative of Early Carolina", p. 114; O: 97 P: 67...
Mauley, Jno.	Taylor			A: 178; D: 87
Maverick, John James Towne 1672	Parliament (1672), Overseer for T. Colleton and J. Stroud, Merchant	Barbados Feb. 1670/71 on the *John and Thomas*	3 Servants	A: 53, 79, 120, 131, 189; C: 42, 43, 45, 57, 58; D: 83; F: 7...; G: 73; H: 274...; L: 155; P: 70
May, John	Servant	Apr. 1670		A: 60
Maybank, David (Sr.) died before Dec. 12, 1682 David Maybank (Jr.) Oyster Point	Carpenter	Before Oct. 1678		A: 181, 192; D: 44, 245; G: 23, 64; H: 457

NAME, OTHERS IN FAMILY, TOWN SETTLED IN	OCCUPATION AND TITLE	SERVANTS AND SLAVES	PLACE OF ORIGIN AND DATE OF ARRIVAL	SOURCES
Mayoh, Edward (Sr.) Wife, Ann (1683) Oyster Point Quaker	Deputy Register of the Province		Before Apr. 1678	A: 155, 158, 168, 190; B: 140, 164; D: 44, 119; E: 1, 5, 29, 51, 76, 81, 107, 110, 289; G: 38, 39, 138, 144, 168, 216; N: 2, 4
Mayoh, Robert Oyster Point			Before May 1678	A: 158
Meader, John Wife, Mary Son, John Oyster Point	Blockmaker, Blacksmith, Gentleman			A: 189, 200; D: 80; E: 68, 70, 75, 114, 194; G: 15, 84, 183, 215, 216, 253
Meadlin (Medlin), Richard Wife, Rachel	Mason			A: 167; D: 93; G: 35
Mells, John Wife, Elizabeth	Freeman			A: 128
Mercer, Alexander	Freeman			A: 163
Michell, John Oyster Point			Bermuda Before Apr. 1679	A: 139, 198; D: 80
Middleton, Arthur	Gentleman, Esquire, Lord Proprietor's Deputy, Naval Officer		Barbados Aug. 1679 (Sailed on Barq *Plantacon* from Barbados)	A: 173; B: 15, 35, 76...; E: 85, 133, 149, 154, 232; G: 16; J: 391; L: 184, 205, 210, 224; P: 246...

51

Name	Occupation/Status	Origin/Date	References
Middleton, Edward died before Aug. 21, 1685 Wife, Sarah, widow of Richard Fowell Oyster Point	Grand Council, Gentleman, Part owner of the *Mary*	Before Sept. 7, 1678	A: 173; B: 9, 13; D: 120; E: 45, 133, 134, 161, 163, 185, 210; F: 83; G: 16, 36, 37 (Charter), 58, 228; J: 304; N: 2, 3
Middleton, Thomas Wife, Elizabeth	2 Servants	England First Fleet on *Carolina*	H: 135; J: 337; O: 97 Apparently did not come
Midwinter, Thomas died before Mar. 26, 1683 Wife and Son (New) Charles Towne 1682	Cooper, Wine Cooper	Before Sept. 5, 1674	A: 81, 166, 207; E: 29; G: 8, 21, 24, 103, 109, 126, 164
Miller, Charles Charles Towne, Lot 46		"One of the first settlers"	A: 194; D: 124; F: 41; See Spanisl Letters, So. Car. Hist. Mag., Vol 3 p. 96
Miller, George Jane, Martha and John Miller, Jr.	Freeman		A: 194
Miller, John	Gentleman		A: 194
Millionton, Richard	Servant to John Smith		A: 106
Mills, John Brother, Henry Mills	Servant to Amos Jefford	Dec. 1671	A: 76, 77; G: 227
Ming, Daniel	Seaman on *Blessing*, Mariner		F: 4

NAME, OTHERS IN FAMILY, TOWN SETTLED IN	OCCUPATION AND TITLE	SERVANTS AND SLAVES	PLACE OF ORIGIN AND DATE OF ARRIVAL	SOURCES
Montgomery, James	Servant to O'Sullivan		England First Fleet on *Carolina*	H: 134
Moore, James died of Distemper before Mar. 1706/07 James Moore Jr.	Captain, Esquire, Gentleman, Lord Proprietor's Deputy, Secretary of Province, Governor, Receiver General, Chief Justice	37 Servants Arr. on his account c. Aug., 1684	Before Apr. 20, 1677	D: 121, 228, 245; E: 10A, 72, 159, 184, 188, 232, 372A; F: 74, 76, 81-84; G: 23, 36 (Charter of the *Mary*), 73, 102, 118, 136, 198, 222, 231; I: 448, 452; L: 12...; N: 3; P: 20...
Moore, John died before 1672	Mariner, Seaman on *Carolina*		Before Sept. 14, 1670	A: 28; E: 91; H: 141: P: 35
Moran, Michael died before Nov. 1672 Wife and Child			Ireland First Fleet	A: 52, 105
Morgan, John See Edward Wallington	Planter		Barbados (?) Feb. 1670/71	A: 88; B: 170; L: 208; M: Vol. 10, p. 240; N: 1; O: 934 (?)
Morgan, Richard	Servant to John Fallock, Freeman before Aug. 1677		Mar. 1674	A: 68, 139
Moron (Moran), Denis Wife and Child			Aug. 1672	A: 73
Morrill, William Son, John Morrill		3 Servants	Dec. 1671	A: 41, 67, 97 Further study needed on Morrill, Murrill, Murharle

Name	Notes	Origin/Date	References
Morris, Mary		Dec. 1678	B: 98
Morris, Morgan		Virginia	A: 128; B: 148, 149; E: 344,
married Sarah Hill		Dec. 1671	346; H: 355
Morris, Samuel	Servant to Hambleton, Seaman on Ketch *Fellowship* (Jan. 1674)	England First Fleet on *Carolina*	C: 53; H: 135
Morrison, Tresimus	Servant to Thomas Lane	Jamaica (?) May 1673	A: 64, 75
Motteshed, Thomas		England First Fleet on *Carolina*	H: 136; O: 97 Apparently did not arrive or died
Mullrayne, James O. Wife, Marie			A: 200
Munkester (Munkister), Thomas Wife, Mary Ran away Jan. 1672			F: 25; H: 329
Murrell, John			D: 64; E: 268; J: 456; L: 172
Murrill, William Oyster Point	Planter, Gentleman		A: 123, 132, 198; D: 64, 68, 69, 70, 215; F: 37, 62; H: 329; J: 456
Mussells, Edward			D: 80
Musson, Edward Wife, Miriam	Cordwainer, Planter (1679)		A: 180; B: 35; D: 105, 307; E: 33, 54, 55, 56; L: 15

NAME, OTHERS IN FAMILY, TOWN SETTLED IN	OCCUPATION AND TITLE	SERVANTS AND SLAVES	PLACE OF ORIGIN AND DATE OF ARRIVAL	SOURCES
Neale, John		Servant to Henry Hughes, Servant to John Coming	First Fleet	A: 22, 23, 45, 82
Needham, James died on exploring trip 1673?			Before Oct. 14, 1671	C: 21, 28, 29; F: 10, 45; H: 411, 452, 453; K: 1; O: 605, 607
Newball, Paule				A: 179
Newton, Isaac				A: 172
Nichols, John Thomas Linbrey, citizen and clouthworker of London, was heir (1681) to John Nichols	Taylor		England	D: 50, 124; G: 86
Nicklin, Richard		Servant to Col. Joseph West	Before Oct. 1672	F: 47, 48, 49, 62, 63; H: 329
Nicolls, Roger	Freeman			A: 135
Noone, Francis		Servant to Paul and Thomas Smith	England First Fleet	H: 134
Norris, Thomas died before Feb. 2, 1682 Albemarle Point	Owen's Parliament (July 4, 1670)		England First Fleet	A: 56, 76; C: 5, 10, 31, 32, 38, 39; F: 35, 37; G: 6, 56, 57; H: 176; O: 213

Name	Occupation/Role	Notes	Origin/Date	References
Norris, Elizabeth	Servant to Christopher Portman		Aug. 1671 on *Blessing*	A: 113
Norton, John (Sr.) Son, John Oyster Point	Captain, Turner, Joyner	Negro Emanuell	by Feb. 1670/71	A: 185; C: 22, 32-33, 55, 56; D: 68, 69, 89; E: 18A, 283; F: 5, 7, 43, 44, 65, 66; G: 104, 172, 174; L: 126
Norvill, Thomas (Took part in William Hilton's Voyage 1664)			Barbados	A: 42; C: 16; H: 30
Norwood, Andrew	Gentleman		Bermuda (?)	C: 45-48, 50-51
Ohohi, Patrick				A: 205
Oldys, Joseph	Deputy Secretary, Deputy Register		Before Nov. 11, 1671	B: 66, 182, 183; C: 24, 30, 31, 63; D: 109, 194; E: 139, 267; F: 13, 14
Orrill, Philip	Servant to John Coming, Planter		Aug. 1671 on *Blessing*	A: 45, 135; L: 137
O'Sullivan, Florence Charles Towne, Lots 5, 6, 26 and 27	Gentleman, Captain, Parliament (1672), Surveyor General, Lord Proprietor's Deputy (?)	16 Servants	St. Margaret, Westminster, First Fleet on *Carolina*	A: 37, 38, 44, 52, 104, 105, 190; C: 8, 9, 45-48, 50, 59, 61; E: 77, 284; F: 5, 16, 17, 30, 36, 39, 40, 42, 49, 71; G: 2, 3, 193, 244; H: 134...; O: 55...
Ottaway, Edward	Seaman			F: 4
Owen, Morgan	Servant to Thomas Dickinson		Sept. 1675	A: 108

NAME, OTHERS IN FAMILY, TOWN SETTLED IN	OCCUPATION AND TITLE	SERVANTS AND SLAVES	PLACE OF ORIGIN AND DATE OF ARRIVAL	SOURCES
Owen, William died before Mar. 27, 1683 Charles Towne, Lots 23 and 32	Gentleman, Esquire, Grand Council, Lord Proprietor's Deputy (1682), Owen's Parliament	5 Servants	England First Fleet on *Carolina*	A: 16, 17, 18, 56, 185, 208...; B: 3...; C: 5, 38, 52, 65; E: 23A; F: 3...; G: 23, 24, 156; H: 135...; O: 97...
Paige (Page), William			Before Aug. 1679	A: 204; D: 97; E: 112, 356; L: 120
Paine (Payne), Robert	Seaman			D: 29
Parker, Paul	Merchant, Gentleman		Sept. 1677	A: 144, 172; D: 177, 230, 235; G: 7, 149, 210; K: 14; L: 37
Parker, Thomas	Servant to Col. William Sayle		Bermuda (?) Sept. 1670	A: 52
Patterson, Thomas	Servant (2 years), Carpenter		Barbados Feb. 16, 1671 on *Carolina*	H: 253
Paty, Eliza			Barbados Jan. 1678 Ship *Joseph and Ann*	J: 393
Paty, Theophilus Oyster Point	Esquire, Cooper		Before Apr. 1678	A: 156, 161, 166, 170; D: 145, 147; E: 62, 87; G: 140, 193, 208; L: 129
Payne, Agnes	Servant to Hambleton		England First Fleet on *Carolina*	H: 135

Name	Arrival / Origin	Servants	Status / Occupation	References
Peele, Francis	Before June 1679		Freeman	A: 201
Pendarvis, Joseph / Wife, Elizabeth and her daughter, Precilla / Son, John / Daughters, Mary and Ann / Charles Towne, Lot 45	First Fleet		Planter (1676), Gentleman (1694)	A: 25, 26, 34, 68, 111; B: 31, 33; D: 14, 48, 236, 237, 258; E: 170, 230, 239, 249; F: 41, 51; G: 234; L: 5; N: 1, 3
Penderry, Thomas			Servant to John Smith	A: 105, 106
Peper, Vera Aurora married Thomas Hurst before 1675?				A: 179; D: 124
Percevall, Andrew / Wife, Essex / Daughter, Mary / Sons, Andrew and James	Westminster, County Middlesex, England 1674	2 Servants	Merchant, Colonel, Esquire, Lord Proprietor's Deputy to Duke of Albemarle, Grand Council, Register of the Province (1675), relative of Lord Shaftesbury	A: 125, 160... (Percival); B: 63, 64, 68, 129, 162; D: 1, 99, 177, 178, 235; E: 32, 70, 76, 124, 139, 357, 360, 372A, 380; F: 78, 79, 80, 82, 83, 85; G: 19, 34, 50, 161, 188, 202, 219, 254, 257; H: 439...; I: 316, 388; K: 22; L: 19...; O: 721...; P: 20, 35
Perriman (Perryman), Augustine / Wife, Ann				A: 174
Perriman, William / Son, William Perriman, Jr. of age by 1684				A: 206; E: 147; G: 231, 233; L: 166
Perry, Edward	Sept. 1675		Servant to Thomas Butler	A: 112; L: 105

NAME, OTHERS IN FAMILY, TOWN SETTLED IN	OCCUPATION AND TITLE	SERVANTS AND SLAVES	PLACE OF ORIGIN AND DATE OF ARRIVAL	SOURCES
Pett, Robert	Servant to Robert Browne		Aug. 1672	A: 110, 114
Phillips, Abra	Servant to Maurice Mathews		England First Fleet on *Carolina*	H; 134
Pierce, Richard Wife, Christian			Feb. 1670/71 (?)	B: 60, 111
Pile, William			Barbados Barque *Susanna* 1678	J: 394
Pinkard (Pinchert, Pinckett, Pincard), John Wife, Mary Son, John Pinckett, Jr. Arr. Aug. 1672 Charles Towne, Lot 36	Elected to Parliament (1672)	1 Servant	June 1671	A: 31, 90; C: 34...; D: 124; F: 30, 41, 59, 60, 67, 68, 69, 73; G: 2
Pinke, John Charles Towne, Lot 36	Cooper, "Viewer of pipestaves"	1 Servant	Barbados Feb. 1670/71	A: 51; C: 11, 41, 45, 55, 56; F: 17, 66; J: 395
Pitt, Josias Wife, Rebecca, daughter of William Thomas, late of Virginia, Gentleman	Planter, Gentleman		Bermuda	E: 280, 282; F: 80

Name	Occupation / Notes	Servants	Origin / Arrival	References
Plummer, Richard	Seaman		England First Fleet	F: 4
Pocock, Judith	Servant to Edward Mathews		Aug. 1671 on *Blessing*	A: 113
Poole, Thomas	Servant to John Rivers		England First Fleet on *Carolina*	H: 135
Poore, Richard	Servant to J. Foster and Thomas Gray, Sawyer		Barbados Feb. 1670/71 on *Carolina*	A: 10, 28, 30; C: 25; H: 253, 364
Popple (Peple), Magnus by 1686 he had returned to Barbados	Shipwright, Commander Barque *Return* which he sold in 1683, also interest in the *Mary* in 1686		Barbados Oct. 1679 on *Endeavor*	E: 10A, 11A, 72, 167, 250; G: 89, 101; J: 398
Porter, William Wife, Margaret				B: 5
Portman, Christopher Charles Towne, Lot 4	Gentleman, Parliament (1672), Grand Council	4 Servants	Aug. 1671 on *Blessing* (Oct. 1679, a passenger on the *Endeavor* from Barbados)	A: 16, 92, 113, 129; C: 52; H: 141...; J: 398
Powell, James	Servant to J. Foster and Thomas Gray, Taylor, Planter (1676)		June 1671	A: 93; C: 25; D: 42, 82, 85; H: 253; N: 1
Powell, Martha			England First Fleet on *Carolina*	H: 136; O: 97
Prettye (Pretye), Henry Charles Towne, Lot 56	Ensign		England Apr. 1672	A: 40; C: 48, 59, 60-61; F: 41; H: 448, 449...; O: 1293...

NAME, OTHERS IN FAMILY, TOWN SETTLED IN	OCCUPATION AND TITLE	SERVANTS AND SLAVES	PLACE OF ORIGIN AND DATE OF ARRIVAL	SOURCES
Price, Henry	Servant to Joseph Dalton		England First Fleet on *Carolina*	H: 134; J: 457
Price, Stephen	Servant to Nicholas Cartwright		England First Fleet on *Carolina*	H: 135
Prideox, George	Servant to Joseph Dalton		England First Fleet on *Carolina*	A: 24; H: 134
Pulford, Joane				A: 147
Pursell, Edmund	Servant to John Williamson		England First Fleet	A: 27
Purvey, James	Servant to John Pinckett		Aug. 1672	A: 31, 90
Quintin (Quintyne), Richard Wife, Elizabeth	Gentleman		Barbados Aug. 1679 on *Plantacon*	A: 193, 210; B: 133; D: 135; E: 23A, 320, 321; G: 131; J: 398; K: 36 (Will); M: Vol. 8, p. 195
Radcliffe, John	Servant to Thomas Gray and J. Foster (2 years)		Barbados Feb. 16, 1670/71 on *Carolina*	C: 25; F: 22, 23, 50; H: 254

Name	Occupation / Status	Origin / Date	References
Ravens, John Ruth Wallen, now his wife (1684)	Servant	Apr. 1672	B: 81, 148; L: 95...
Read, Lawrence Oyster Point Lot 14 (1679)	Merchant		E: 25A, 45
Reade (Reed), Thomas	Servant to Jacob Wayte, Freeman by 1681	Sept. 1675	A: 104; D: 143 (Grant of 70 Acres, 1681)
Reade, William	Merchant, Ship *Endeavour*	Boston	D: 151, 152; E: 56, 168, 277 Did not seem to settle here.
Reed, Jo	Servant to Hambleton	England First Fleet on *Carolina*	II: 135
Reese, Bartholomew	Esquire, "Barbados Adventurer"	Barbados Before Sept. 1672	A?: 42; C: 18; II: 254; J: 471
Reese, John	Servant to William Owens	Barbados (?) Feb. 1670/71	A: 56
Rewbery, George Wife, Elizabeth		June 1671	A: 84; B: 177
Rich, Richard	Planter		G: 61 (Inventory), 62 (Will)
Richardson, Robert James Towne		Before July 1672	A: 21; II: 30
Richmond, Andrew		June 1671	A: 89; G: 98

NAME, OTHERS IN FAMILY, TOWN SETTLED IN	OCCUPATION AND TITLE	SERVANTS AND SLAVES	PLACE OF ORIGIN AND DATE OF ARRIVAL	SOURCES
Rideal, Thomas			England First Fleet on *Carolina*	H: 136; O: 97 Apparently never arrived
Right, Robert	Master Ship *Betty* of Carolina		Nov. 1678	B: 103; E: 188; G: 91, 128
Rilley, Charles Colony of James Towne	Servant to Col. William Sayle		Sept. 1670	A: 52, 61
Rivers, John	Servant to Richard Cole		Aug. 1671 on *Blessing*	A: 55; F: 14, 47, 48, 49 Apparently did not take up land.
Rivers, John Kinsman of Lord Ashley	Agent for Lord Ashley	4 Servants (3 probably died or returned)	England First Fleet on *Carolina*	H: 127, 135, 205; I: 344; O: 89 Apparently he did not take up land. Bull asked for his job Sept. 1670.
Rivers, Moses				A: 205
Rixam, Mrs. Jane Daughter		2 Servants	1676	A: 118
Rix, Alice	Servant to Thomas and Paul Smith		England First Fleet on *Carolina*	A: 96; H: 134
Roades, Will	Servant to Joseph Dalton		England First Fleet on *Carolina*	A: 24; H: 134

Name	Notes	Servants/Slaves	Arrival	References
Roberts, Edward			Barbados, Feb. 1670/71	A: 50, 103, 462; C: 21; K: 1
Roberts, George	Servant to Col. William Sayle		First Fleet	A: 52, 61
Robinson, James				A: 22; L: 212
Robinson, Mrs. Jane		1 Negro Grace	Barbados (?) Feb. 1670/71	A: 54
Robinson, John Charles Towne, Lot 47	Captain, Parliament (1672-June 1673), Grand Council (1672)	1 Negro Yackae	Barbados (?) Feb. 1670/71	A: 16, 54; C: 5, 49; F: 30...; J: 465; O: 120...
Robry, John	Servant to Robert Gough		July 1672	A: 48, 148
Rose, Thomas died before 1687 Oyster Point (1680) (Lot sold by executors to Thomas Smith)	Provost Marshall (1680)	Several Servants	Before 1677 (?)	A: 129; 208; B: 22, 154, 210; D: 146, 149, 185; E: 28A; G: 23, 79; 80; L: 21, 170; N: 2, 34; See McCrady Plats, Case 437, Charleston County Court House
Rowntree, Thomas			May 1674	A: 108; D: 46, 215
Rowser, Richard died before Dec. 4, 1683 Wife, Mary Son, Richard Rowser	Servant to John Maverick	1 man servant Arr. Feb. 1681/82	Before Sept. 9, 1671	A: 83, 211; B: 136; D: 197; E: 63; F: 7; G: 2, 196, 200
Saker, George	Servant to John Pinke		Barbados Feb. 1670/71	A: 51

188

NAME, OTHERS IN FAMILY, TOWN SETTLED IN	OCCUPATION AND TITLE	SERVANTS AND SLAVES	PLACE OF ORIGIN AND DATE OF ARRIVAL	SOURCES
Sanders, Lawrence			Before 1678	A: 152, 206; B: 67; G: 137
Sayle, James	Captain		Bermuda	A: 52, 61; C: 40; F: 80; H: 280
Sayle, Nathaniel Charles Towne Lots 59 and 60	Captain, Receiver General	4 Negroes 4 Servants	Bermuda Sept. 1670	A: 52, 61; C: 39, 40; D: 77; F: 19, 40, 41, 54, 80; H: 173...; P: 216
Sayle, William died before Mar. 4, 1671 Sons, Nathaniel and James Mansion House Albemarle Point	Colonel, First Governor, Lord Proprietor's Deputy	1 Servant	Bermuda First Fleet	A: 52, 61; C: 9, 39, 40; F: 19; H: 176...; I: 340, 387; K: 16 (Will); O: 177...
Scantlebury, Jacob				F: 28; H: 30
Sceman, Thomas Charles Towne	Gentleman		Eastcheape, England Before Oct. 1671	C: 14, 16, 30; F: 13, 14
Schenckingh, Barnard Town lots 90 and 70 Oyster Point	Captain, Esquire, Gentleman, Merchant, Sheriff of Berkley Co. (1691), Justice of Peace, Trustee for Granting Land		Barbados Before Dec. 19, 1672	A: 202, 206, 211; B: 16, 24, 44, 72, 146, 159, 202; C: 56-59; D: 149, 184; E: 47, 90, 112, 130A, 142, 147, 154, 360; G: 8, 103, 128, 231, 233, 263; I: 322; J: 458, 490; L: 138, 139; M: Vol. 8, p. 197; N: 4; P: 18, 28, 72

Name	Status/Notes	Origin & Date	References
Scott, Jno	Servant to O'Sullivan	England, First Fleet	A: 37, 104
Scrawhall, Dermott	Servant to Thomas Gray	Barbados (?), Feb. or June 1671	A: 28
Scrivener, William died before Dec. 1671	Grand Council (Sept. 1670), Doctor, Lord Proprietor's Deputy, 1 Servant	England, First Fleet	A: 17, 18, 56; H: 135…
Seabrook, Robert	Merchant, Shaftesbury gave him Power of Attorney (1682), 2 Servants	Before Dec. 29, 1679	B: 12, 29, 102; D: 109, 110, 111; E: 29, 95; G: 122; L: 3…
Searle, Andrew	Servant to Samuel West	England, First Fleet on *Carolina*	A: 27; H: 136
Searle, Richard / Wife, Mary Oyster Point, Lot 12 (1682)	Gentleman	Before Dec. 1679	A: 193; B: 11; E: 45, 77, 107, 222; G: 21; L: 67
Serjeant, Richard		Barbados, Jan. 1678, Ship *Joseph and Ann*	J: 402
Serles, Thomas Oyster Point	Gentleman	Barbados (?)	A: 156; J: 441, 489
Sessions, Robert Wife and Son		July 11, 1678	B: 126

NAME, OTHERS IN FAMILY, TOWN SETTLED IN	OCCUPATION AND TITLE	SERVANTS AND SLAVES	PLACE OF ORIGIN AND DATE OF ARRIVAL	SOURCES
Shaftesbury, Anthony Ashley Cooper (See Ashley)	Earl, Lord Proprietor			A: 103, 119, 120; D: 12; F: 57, 75, 76, 79; H: 339...; L: 9...; N: 1; P: 81
Shaw, Thomas — Wife, Katherine	Captain, Mariner, Commander Barque *Endeavor*, Gentleman	Servants	Before 1677	A: 149; B: 9, 79, 130; D: 113, 144; E: 10A; L: 55; O: 512
Shepherd, Agnes				F: 68
Shepherd, John				A: 195, 201; G: 9; L: 112, 150
Sherdon, Hugh	Servant		Sept. 1672	A: 35
Shory (Shoris), Anthony Oyster Point, Lot 26 Left the Province for Barbados by 1687	Cooper		Before May 1678	A: 161, 165; E: 39, 43, 97, 98, 294, 298; G: 110, 134; L: 23; M: Vol. 8, p. 206
Shurgeron, Teige	Servant to O'Sullivan			A: 37, 104
Simonds, Henry (See Symonds)			England First Fleet	
Simpson (Sympson), John Wife, Margaret Son, Richard Arr. Sept. 1675	Freeman, Carpenter		Dec. 13, 1671	A: 128; B: 148, 149; F: 50, 65, 76; G: 192 (Inventory of his wife)

Name	Status/Occupation	Origin	Servants	References
Slaughter, William	Servant to John Jennings			J: 402
Smallwood, Mathew Wife, Ann	Servant to John Rivers (1670), Freeman by 1674, Planter (1681)	England First Fleet on *Carolina*		A: 88, 147; E: 16A, 20A, 21A; F: 72; G: 54; H: 135; L: 188, 193
Smethwick, Daniel				A: 150
Smethwick, Robert Oyster Point				A: 151, 165, 169
Smith, Abraham died before Aug. 1694 Wife, Hannah	Servant to Will Bowman (1670), Servant to Col. Joseph West, Freeman by Aug. 1677, Bricklayer (1678)	England First Fleet on *Carolina*		A: 63, 141, 186; B: 6; D: 83, 89, 117, 138, 185, 304; E: 29; G: 55; H: 135; L: 41, 42
Smith, Christopher Wife, Jane Wife, Dorothy Sons, John, Ralph Grandson, Christopher Granddaughter, Mary Beresford	Merchant, Gentleman	Bermuda		D: 124, 188; E: 50, 86; G: 82, 69; J: 429 (Barbados); K: 24 (Will); L: 164, 180
Smith, Mrs. Dorcas died before Jan. 2, 1683/84		1672 and 1673	1 Negro Man 2 Women Servants	A: 60, 87; B: 143; D: 53
Smith, Edward		Barbados Mar. 1678 on Bark *Susanna*		J: 403; L: 66,143

NAME, OTHERS IN FAMILY, TOWN SETTLED IN	OCCUPATION AND TITLE	SERVANTS AND SLAVES	PLACE OF ORIGIN AND DATE OF ARRIVAL	SOURCES
Smith, Elizabeth	Servant to Thomas and Paul Smith		England First Fleet on *Carolina*	A: 48; H: 134
Smith, Hester			Barbados Feb. 1678	J: 403
Smith, James Charles Towne Lots 41 and 57 Associated with Thomas Smith	Merchant	4 Servants	Before May 1672	A: 9, 16, 96; C: 54; E: 233; F: 41; L: 170; O: 954 (?)
Smith (Smyth), John Wife, Mary	Merchant, Cassique, Esquire, Grand Council, Lord Proprietor's Deptuy (July 1677)	Brought 7 Servants. When he died he had: 3 White, 9 Negro and 4 Indian	Before Oct. 1675	A: 105, 106, 110; C: 64, 65; D: 18; F: 77, 82, 84; G: 21, 22 (Inventory), 53, 219; H: 457...; I: 452; N: 1
Smith, Mitchael (Michael) James Towne 1672 Charles Towne Lot 38 (1672)	Merchant		New York (1671)	C: 13, 14, 42, 43; F: 18, 41 (May have left Carolina early)
Smith, Paule died before June 25, 1672 Associated with Thomas Smith	"Preacher," Grand Council (Mar. 1670-Aug. 1671)		England First Fleet on *Carolina*	A: 16, 17, 48; C: 39, 40, 41; H: 134; K: 17; L: 168; O: 97
Smith, Robert	Servant to John Smith			A: 106

Name	Occupation/Role	Servants	Origin/Arrival	References
Smith, Robert Father, Henry Smith of Parish of St. Michaells in the County of Hartford	Merchant (1677), Planter		England	A: 143; D: 74, 100, 177; E: 232; G: 210
Smith, Roger	Carpenter			A: 182
Smith (Smyth), Thomas Charles Towne Lots 41 and 57	Owen's Parliament, Gentleman (1675, 1687), Esquire (1689, 1694), Merchant (1688), Justice of Peace (1689), Lord Proprietor's Deputy, Landgrave, Governor	7 Servants	England First Fleet on *Carolina*	A: 9, 16, 66, 95, 96; C: 15, 54; D: 194, 200, 202, 207, 209; E: 82 (Jan. 1682), 84, 208, 267, 277, 299, 309, 372A; F: 41; G: 1, 72; H: 134; L: 170...; O: 97...; P: 18... (?) **Further study needed on Thomas Smiths.**
Smith, Thomas	Servant to Captain John Godfrey and Colletons		Apr. 1672	A: 4
Smyth, Thomas	Doctor (?), One of the Freeman (1677)		Before 1677	A: 137
Snipes, William died before Mar. 1677 Wife, Margaret Son, Thomas	Carpenter		Barbados Before Feb. 1677	G: 65 (Will 1677); J: 461
Southell, Thomas	Servant to Hambleton		England First Fleet on *Carolina*	H: 135
Spencer, Oliver Oyster Point	Blacksmith	4 Servants Arr. June 1671	Aug. 1672	A: 38, 84, 148, 154; D: 237; E: 207; F: 58, 59, 73; G: 2, 200; H: 456...; L: 62, 117, 211

NAME, OTHERS IN FAMILY, TOWN SETTLED IN	OCCUPATION AND TITLE	SERVANTS AND SLAVES	PLACE OF ORIGIN AND DATE OF ARRIVAL	SOURCES
Stanyarne, James Father, Thomas Stanyarne Quaker			May 1675	D: 46, 57; E: 57; L: 38...; M: Vol. 8, p. 167; P: 104
Stanyarne (Stanyan), Thomas died before Apr. 17, 1683 Wife, Mary Sons, James, Thomas, William Daughter, Mary Ladson Quaker	Tanner, Merchant	4 Servants	May 1675	A: 122, 127; D: 46, 57, 59; E: 22A; G: 144; K: 3; L: 147, 166, 195; N: 1, 3
Steere, Thomas	Servant to Edward Mathews		Aug. 1671 on *Blessing*	A: 64, 101, 113; C: 52
Stevens, John	Cooper			A: 168; B: 49, 150, 159, 187, 189; D: 134; E: 198; L: 75...; M: Vol. 10, p. 236
Stevenson, Elinor She married William Wilkinson before 1684	Servant to Capt. John Comings		Aug. 1679	B: 154
Stevenson, John Oyster Point			Jamaica (?) Before Apr. 21, 1677	A: 130, 158, 162, 168; B: 34; D: 26; O: 99
Stevenson, Tho				A: 134

Name	Occupation	Notes	Origin / Arrival	References
Steward (Stuard), Patrick / Wife, Margaret	Servant (1673), Freeman by Sept. 1674		Jamaica (?) May 1673	A: 87, 98; C: 56, 59, 61, 67, 68, 69; E: 268; G: 174, 176, 188, 244; L: 121, 197
Stock, John	Freeman		Aug. 1671 on *Blessing*	A: 183; G: 65; L: 180, 237
Stonehall, Elizabeth	Servant to Thomas Hurt		Aug. 1671 on *Blessing*	A: 34, 68
Stranton, Elinor	Servant to Thomas Smith		Feb. 1672	A: 66
Strode (Stroud), John	Merchant, In business venture with T. Colleton, Part owner the *John and Thomas*	20 Servants in Partnership with H. Harvey Arr. Feb. 8, 1671 on the *John and Thomas*	Barbados Before Nov. 1670	C: 53, 56, 59, 83; H: 212...; J: 458, 505; L: 91...
Stryde, John	Servant to Richard Cole		Aug. 1671 on *Blessing*	A: 55
Sturman, George				G: 64 (Inventory 1678)
Sullivan, Margaret				A: 72
Sullivan, Daniel	Servant to O'Sullivan		England First Fleet	A: 37, 104; L: 163
Sullivan, John died before Jan. 15, 1692/93 Wife, Racholl	Planter		England First Fleet	A: 32, 63, 157, 161; C: 60, 61, 157, 161; D: 124; E: 40A; F: 66; G: 61; L: 170; M: Vol. 8, p. 165, 170
Sullivan, Timothy			1679	B: 149; L: 135, 168

NAME, OTHERS IN FAMILY, TOWN SETTLED IN	OCCUPATION AND TITLE	SERVANTS AND SLAVES	PLACE OF ORIGIN AND DATE OF ARRIVAL	SOURCES
Sumers, Thomas Charles Towne (Sept. 14, 1670) (The only deed found to Charles Towne lot)	Mariner, Seaman on *Carolina*			E: 91; H: 141, 241; L: 208
Sumpton, Henry Wife, Susanah	Servant to Thomas and James Smith, Freeman by Feb. 1677/78		Aug. 1671 on *Blessing*	A: 9, 96, 151; G: 63
Sumpton, Thomas				D: 101
Swade (Swaine), Christopher Lot at "Kaiawah, formerly called Charles Towne" (Sept. 25, 1684)	Servant to Will Owens, Freeman (1674), Blacksmith		England First Fleet on *Carolina*	A: 56, 69; B: 37, 38; H: 135
Swaine, Thomas Oyster Point (1678)			Jamaica (?)	A: 156, 175; O: 100
Symonds (Simons, Simonds), Henry Wife, Frances	Captain, Planter, Vintner, Victualler, Owen's Parliament		Barbados He arr. Apr. 1670 She arr. Aug. 1671 on *Blessing*	A: 25, 35, 89; B: 33, 194; C: 13, 14, 18, 19, 43, 44, 45; D: 42, 109, 200?; E: 28A, 168, 170, 177, 244, 248; G: 204; K: 35 (Will); L: 11...; O: 213
Sympson, Alexander Oyster Point (1679)	Freeman		Before 1677	A: 169, 207; D: 30

Name	Description	Origin	Servants/Family	References
Sympson, John				A: 128
Taprill, Robert				F: 65
Taylor, Stephen	Servant to Amos Jefford	Dec. 1671		A: 76
Terry, John James Towne				A: 18; D: 52
Thomas, Alice	Servant to John Culpeper	Dec. 1671		A: 53
Thomas, John Wife		Jamaica (?)	Several Servants	A: 154; L: 180; O: 102
Thomas, Robert Wife, Mary	Servant to Thomas Clutterbuck, Freeman (1675)	Barbados (?) Feb. 1671		A: 15, 100
Thomas, William died before 1679 Wife, Mary Daughter, Rebecca, married Josiah Pitt	Gentleman (1676)	Northumberland Co. Virginia Aug. 13, 1677	2 Negroes 5 Servants 1 Child	A: 61, 62, 113; E: 280; F: 75; G: 41 (Died before 1679)
Thompson, George Charles Towne Lots 16 and 17 Wife, Grissell	Captain, Merchant, Treasurer of "Barbados Adventurers", Provost Marshal, Grand Council	Barbados		A: 8, 71; C: 6, 7, 16, 17, 22, 23, 30, 36, 53, 55, 64; D: 53, 72; F: 34, 36, 41, 46, 67, 71, 72, 73, 74; H: 53, 274
Thompson, John	Servant to Hambleton	England First Fleet on *Carolina*		H: 135

NAME, OTHERS IN FAMILY, TOWN SETTLED IN	OCCUPATION AND TITLE	SERVANTS AND SLAVES	PLACE OF ORIGIN AND DATE OF ARRIVAL	SOURCES
Thompson, Thomas Wife, Sarah Charles Towne, Lot 55	Marshall (1671-1673), Taylor, Gentleman (1675)		Barbados "One of the First Settlers"	A: 24, 25, 139; C: 11, 18, 19, 21, 28; D: 31, 55; F: 11, 23, 29, 34, 41; G: 2; H: 302, 339...
Thrush, John	Freeman			A: 200
Titus	Captain, Indian Interpreter			F: 80; O: 225...
Tomes, Robert Wife	Planter			A: 140; E: 240
Tothill (Toble), John died before Aug. 15, 1684 Wife, Sarah Daughter, Sara Tothill, Jr. of age but unmarried (Aug. 1684)	Planter, Esquire, "Barbados Adventurers"	11 Servants Arr. Aug. 1683	Barbados	B: 108, 118; C: 36; D: 64, 70; E: 147; G: 173, 231, 233; H: 29...; J: 447 (?); L: 174
Trad, Richard Oyster Point, Lot 7	Joyner		Before Aug. 1678	A: 169; D: 142, 256; E: 275, 277; L: 15, 98, 167
Trade, Thomas				N: 3
Trott, Perient	Merchant			D: 133; G: 36, 155; N: 2; O: 1154
Trott, Samuel	Merchant		Somers Island Bermuda	D: 133 (1679); G: 36, 155; N: 2

Name		Occupation / Notes	Origin / Date	Reference
Tucke, William		Seaman on Ketch *Fellowship* (1674), Servant to Joseph West	Somers Island Bermuda	C: 53
Tuder, Margaret		Servant to Dr. William Scrivener	England First Fleet on *Carolina*	H: 135
Turpin, Thomas died before 1681 Charles Towne, Lot 33	1 Servant		Apr. 1671	A: 49, 124, 176; C: 55, 56; F: 41; G: 5
Turner, Daniel		Carpenter	England c. Aug. 1678	So. Car. Hist. Mag., Vol. 37, p. 137
Val, John			England c. Oct. 1679	So. Car. Hist. Mag., Vol. 37, p. 138
Vale (Vide), Thomas Age c. 40 (1674)		Servant to James and Thomas Smith	Aug. 1671 on *Blessing*	A: 9, 96; So. Car. Hist. Mag., Vol. 37, p. 95
Varbin, Joseph				A: 160
Vaughan, Ann			Aug. 24, 1676	B: 149
Vincum, Violetta		Servant to John Smith		A: 105
Wade, John Oyster Point		Colonel, Planter (1678)	Before Sept. 1676	A: 117, 159; D: 26; G: 2, 44

NAME, OTHERS IN FAMILY, TOWN SETTLED IN	OCCUPATION AND TITLE	SERVANTS AND SLAVES	PLACE OF ORIGIN AND DATE OF ARRIVAL	SOURCES
Wadeland, Thomas	Seaman on *Blessing* (1670), Commander of Pink *Desire* (1678)			C: 31, 32, 46; F: 4; J: 370
Waight, Jacob Wife, Sarah Son Oyster Point Lots 13 and 16 Quaker	Leathercutter (1676), Cordwainer (1682), Vintnor (1688)	3 Servants	1675 *The Edista* Lord Shaftesbury's Dogger	A: 104, 106, 157; B: 151, 153, 173, 174, 175; D: 43, 91; E: 22A, 30, 99, 101, 111, 112; F: 78; G: 86, 234; H: 464, 465; K: 14
Walker, John Wife, Mary	Freeman, Carpenter		Jamaica (?)	A: 179; B: 61, 68; G: 230; O: 101
Walley, William	Captain, Esquire (1681), Owned Plantation 1677			A: 164; B: 42; F: 81, 82, 83
Wallington, Edward died before July 18, 1681 His widow, Elizabeth married John Morgan	Freeman		Before 1677	A: 147; B: 170; E: 165; G: 5
Watkins, John Wife, Ann		1 Servant	England First Fleet	A: 57, 181; D: 41; L: 58, 89
Webb, Nicholas Wife, Elizabeth	Servant to Oliver Spencer, George Rewbery received land for Nicholas Webb (1685)		June 1671	A: 84; B: 177

Name	Description	Servants	Origin	References
Wells, John James Towne			Aug. 1672	A: 39, 40; L: 179
Wells, Richard / Wife, Susan	Servant to William Morrill		Aug. 1672	A: 67
West, Mrs. Joanna			Aug. 1671 on *Blessing*	A: 63
West, Joseph Mrs. West in England 1671 Charles Towne Lots 50, 51, 52, 53 and 62 for Lords Proprietors. Sold *Tryall* in 1683	Landgrave (1674), Merchant (1678), Colonel, Governor (1671), Governor (1674), Governor (1684), Grand Council, Register of Province, Lord Proprietor's Deputy to Earl of Shaftesbury	2 Servants	England, First Fleet	A: 63...; B: 34, 47, 167; D: 8, 194; E: 111, 309, 335; F: 3; G: 50; H: 93...; I: 315, 319, 342, 345, 350, 391...; O: 55...; P: 3...
West, Samuel Charles Towne, Lot 31	Gentleman	2 Servants	England, First Fleet on *Carolina*	A: 27, 76; D: 124, 186; E: 68, 222, 308; F: 30, 34, 40, 62, 65, 68, 70, 71, 72, 74, 75, 77, 79, 80, 82; G: 84, 85; L: 168
West, William	Servant to Samuel West		England, First Fleet on *Carolina*	A: 27; C: 22; H: 136
Westbury, Edward			Jamaica (?)	A: 147; O: 100 (?)
Westbury, William	Servant to John Smith			A: 106; L: 236
Wheelwright, Stephen	Servant to O'Sullivan, Surveyor (1673)		England, First Fleet on *Carolina*	A: 37, 104, 142,...; C: 54, 55; F: 61; H: 134
White, George	Servant to O'Sullivan		First Fleet	A: 37, 104; L: 180

NAME, OTHERS IN FAMILY, TOWN SETTLED IN	OCCUPATION AND TITLE	SERVANTS AND SLAVES	PLACE OF ORIGIN AND DATE OF ARRIVAL	SOURCES
White, Margaret	Free Person			A: 125
White, Phyllis	Servant to Thomas Turpin			A: 124
Whithington, Peleg	Planter		Barbados	A: 161; D: 119; E: 42; G: 71, 159; N: 2
Widzer, Dudley	Servant to Stephen Bull	England First	England, *First Fleet on Carolina*	H: 134
Wigglesworth, Hugh	Servant to Thomas and Paul Smith, Freeman by 1675		England, *First Fleet on Carolina*	A: 96, 107, 195; E: 10A; H: 134
Wigmore, Nathaniel Wife, Ann	Servant to William Morrill, Free Person by Jan. 1678			A: 67, 196
Wilkinson, Henry Junr.	Captain, Cacique, Regerster of Births and Burialls (July 1681)			E: 27A; I: 397; O: 721 B.P.R.O., Col. Entry, Vol. 20, p. 173
Wilkinson, John	Servant to Amos Jefford, Freeman by Apr. 1684		Dec. 1671	A: 76; B: 154
Wilkinson, Will Wife, Elinor Stevenson, Servant to Capt. Comings			Before Aug. 1678	A: 172

Williams, James Wife, Martha	"Chirugen"	England First Fleet	A: 91, 99; B: 37, 94, 185; D: 186; E: 142, 182, 210; G: 198, 199, 206, 211, 213; L: 71...
Williams, John	Servant to William Owens	England First Fleet	A: 56, L: 209, 225
Williams, Robert	Servant to John Rivers	England First Fleet on *Carolina*	G: 164; H: 135
Williams, Thomas Wife, Ellinor Burnet James Towne	Sawyer		A: 11, 47, 118; D: 135, 136; L: 163; N: 2
Williamson, John Wife, Margaret Son, John Daughter, Elizabeth Charles Towne, Lot 7	Mariner	2 Servants	First Fleet	A: 26, 27; E: 19A, 68; G: 98; H: 241; L: 14...
Willis, Elizabeth "New Charles Towne"* Lot 61 (Mar. 13, 1680)			B: 30, 203, 207, 208; D: 132, 189 N:2
Willis, Josiah New Charles Towne Lot 62 (March 15, 1681)	Mariner		B: 23; D: 132; N: 2

*One of the earliest records of the name changing from Oyster Point to Charles Towne.

NAME, OTHERS IN FAMILY, TOWN SETTLED IN	OCCUPATION AND TITLE	SERVANTS AND SLAVES	PLACE OF ORIGIN AND DATE OF ARRIVAL	SOURCES
Willis, Reubin	Carpenter			D: 104; L: 21, 168
Willoughby, James Ran away 1672				F: 25; H: 162
Wilson, Edward Wife, Marieris	Servant to Richard Cole, Freeman by Aug. 1677		Aug. 1671 on *Blessing*	A: 55, 138, 202; J: 487; L: 141; N: 3
Wilson, John	Servant to Jacob Wayte		Sept. 1675	A: 104; C: 63; L: 227
Winthrop, Henry	Servant, Freeman by Dec. 1674		Barbados (?)	A: 79, 93
Wishett, Andrew Wife, Margaret				G: 55
Witter (Whitter), James Wife, Mary	Mariner (1682), Deputy Surveyor (1687)			A: 182; D: 155, 294; E: 10A, 50, 275; G: 7, 35, 101, 246; L: 20...
Witty, Thomas	Servant to John Foster and Thomas Grey (2 years), Sawyer		Barbados Feb. 16, 1670 on *Carolina*	F: 49; H: 253
Wood, Benjamin	Servant to John Boon		Dec. 1671	A: 63; L: 203
Wood, Henry Wife, Alice Charles Towne, Lot 15	Carpenter		England First Fleet	A: 17, 76, 121; C: 21, 36, 37, 39, 55; D: 50, 108, 124; E: 102, 119; F: 41; H: 339

Name	Occupation / Role	Servants / Negroes	Origin / Ship	References
Woodward, Henry Wife, Margaret (Nevis) Wife, Mary, daughter of John Godfrey (June 17, 1681)	Gentleman, Doctor, Lord Proprietor's Deputy	7 Negroes Arr. Nov. 1682	July 8, 1666; Nevis, Apr. 1670 First Fleet	A: 44, 148, 149...; B: 109; C: 11, 12, 13, 44, 148, 149; D: 149 (Wife Mary 1681); E: 2, 3, 26A, 32, 48; F: 45, 83, 84, 85; G: 161; H: 65... (Westo Discovery 1674); I: 316, 390; K: 17
Woodward, Peirce	Merchant			A: 144; E: 3; G: 44
Woodyer (Woodier), Dudley	Servant to Stephen Bull		First Fleet	A: 6, 70
Workeup, Ann	Servant to Samuel Boswood		Aug. 1671 on *Blessing*	A: 19
Works, Robert				D: 104
Worme, Thomas	Servant to Thomas Middleton		England First Fleet on *Carolina*	A: 71; H: 135; L: 121
Wright, Richard	Servant to Thomas Middleton		England First Fleet on *Carolina* Barbados (1679) Mar. 1679 on Ketch *Mary and Sarah* (return trip)	H: 135; J: 414 (1679)
Yarwood, Thomas	Carpenter		Barbados Nov. 1679 on Ship *Endeavor*	G: 101; J: 418
Yeamans, Sir John died Aug. 1674 Charles Towne, Lot 22	Council, Governor (1671), Lord Proprietor's Deputy to Lord Berkeley	1 Servant 8 Negroes	Barbados June 1671	A: 3-80, 85, 91...; C: 11...; D: 2 (Will); F: 3-10, 12, 13, 15, 16, 18, 19, 29, 40, 48, 53, 54, 70, 74, 77 (Will), 81; H: 409...

NAME, OTHERS IN FAMILY, TOWN SETTLED IN	OCCUPATION AND TITLE	SERVANTS AND SLAVES	PLACE OF ORIGIN AND DATE OF ARRIVAL	SOURCES
Yeamans, John James Towne (1674)	Official Surveyor, left Province before Apr. 11, 1684		Barbados	A: 68...; B: 146; D: 42; F: 30, 41, 61, 71, 72-81
Yeamans, Lady Margaret		1 Servant 8 Negroes	Barbados Aug. 1672 and Feb. 1674	A: 82, 112; D: 2, 57, 124; F: 56, 74, 81
Yeamans, Lady Willoughby Widow of Sir William Guardian of son, John Cousin of Sir John			Barbados St. Peters Parish Before 1678	D: 59 (Letter); F: 81; N: 1
Young, Edward	Servant to Hambleton		England First Fleet on *Carolina*	H: 135
Youngborne, Sarah				A: 174, 182
Younge, Thomas	Servant to Joseph Dalton		England First Fleet on *Carolina*	A: 24; H: 134

258